Pre

_____

By

_____

On the Occasion of

_____

Date

_____

LIVE IN VICTORY

PRACTICAL STEPS TO THE OVERCOMING LIFE

CLARENCE L. BLASIER
WITH
REX W. MARSHALL

BARBOUR
PUBLISHING, INC.
Uhrichsville, Ohio

ISBN 1-57748-992-6

All Scripture is taken from the King James Version of the Bible.

Published by Barbour Publishing, Inc., P.O. Box 719, Uhrichsville, OH 44683 http://www.barbourbooks.com

 Member of the
Evangelical Christian
Publishers Association

Printed in the United States of America.

LIVE IN VICTORY

Contents

Introduction

> *For though we walk in the flesh, we do not war after the flesh: (For the weapons of our warfare are not carnal, but mighty through God to the pulling down of strongholds.)*
>
> 2 Corinthians 10:3–4

Reality: Anger, bitterness, inability to forgive, a stressful marriage, pride, envy, discouragement, broken hearts, grief, financial bondage, unplanned pregnancy, physical disability, sexual lust, vengeance, bad temper, homosexuality, obesity, drug addiction, alcoholism, poor health, false religions, loneliness, worshiping idols (such as possessions, wealth, success, pleasure, and so on), depression, selfishness, lying, gossiping, blurred vision of spiritual potential, guilt, betrayal of trust, unethical conduct, limited spiritual perspective, shame.

These are but a few of the undesirable conditions, emotions, or actions we might face, experience, or commit during our lifetime. Some may dominate a person's life for months or even years, and some may spell total destruction.

These "realities" all repress victorious living.

They are strongholds that must be dealt with in order to live in victory as God desires.

If you are battling one or more strongholds, you may feel as if you are losing the fight. Can the battle be won? Can you ever live in victory? The answer is a wonderful, resounding *yes!*

The answer is God gives you assurance that through Him, victory can be yours. Not just hope, but a guaranteed victory! But be careful, and get ready: Your greatest stronghold and your victory over it may not be what you're expecting.

PART I
STRONGHOLDS

What Is a Stronghold?

We usually think of a stronghold as a fortification constructed for defense. For example, Fort Ticonderoga in New York was a stronghold, as is Fort Knox in Kentucky, where gold is stored. However, this is not the type of stronghold the apostle Paul was referring to in 2 Corinthians.

For purposes of our discussion, we will define a stronghold as the following:

- Any ongoing condition that is contrary to the will of a loving and caring God and His plan for our lives;
- Any condition that stands as a barrier between us and a perfect relationship with our Creator;
- Any condition that detracts from and destroys one's spiritual potential;
- Any condition that prevents us from experiencing life more abundantly, which Jesus said He came to bring.

WHO BUILDS
A STRONGHOLD?

This question can best be answered with another question.

Considering our definition of a stronghold, what or who is most likely to bring something into your life that is contrary to the will of a loving and caring God; something that stands as a barrier between you and Him; something that detracts from and destroys your spiritual potential; something that prevents you from living a more abundant life?

Obviously, the enemy of God, Satan!

Paul writes, "Though we walk in the flesh, we do not war after the flesh" (2 Corinthians 10:3), and then he goes on to tell us that our battle is not against flesh and blood, but "against principalities, against powers, against the rulers of the darkness of this world, against spiritual wickedness in high places" (Ephesians 6:12). In other words, our battle is a spiritual war against Satan and his demons!

In his rebellion against God, Satan uses many deceptions and strategies in his dealings with

God's most cherished creation, humankind.

> *Be sober, be vigilant; because your adversary the devil, as a roaring lion, walketh about, seeking whom he may devour.*　　　1 PETER 5:8

Satan began his deception with Adam and Eve in the Garden of Eden and will continue until he is bound for a thousand years and then cast into the lake of fire. (See Revelation 19:19–20.)

Make no mistake about his character: Satan has no compassion. He hates God and he hates every person. He does not hesitate to establish any barrier he possibly can in order to keep us from God and from being used by Him for His purposes. It seems he is especially active against those who defy him and walk in obedience and dedication to the Lord. Because of his determination to destroy us, we can expect to face his strongholds in our life. Satan truly wants to immobilize us, to take us out! But despite his persistence and devious ways, we would be foolish to give Satan all the credit for our problems.

Consider this: LIFE IS NOT ALWAYS FAIR! It was not promised to be, for now, and we must develop an understanding of that principle and grow into an acceptance of it.

Sometimes it even seems like our loving God

is far away, having abandoned us when He really has not. However, learning God's plan and purpose for our lives is the basis for dealing with the seeming unfairness of trials and the accompanying feelings of helplessness and disappointment.

There also are some strongholds that are created because of human nature and poor choices. Our intentions may be good, but often we fail to seek wise counsel, or we get ahead of God or even leave Him out when making decisions. Sometimes we knowingly engage in destructive activities or thoughts, or we are concerned only with the thrill or satisfaction of the moment, failing to consider the long-term consequences of our actions. The result is yet another stronghold.

Furthermore, many of our problems are the result of just being in a sin-filled, fallen world. The cumulative, negative effects of sin must be considered. Since Adam and Eve's first sin there has been a geometric progression of sin that has affected every aspect of human life. If you put a drop of ink into a glass of pure water, the entire contents will become discolored. And as you add more and more ink, before too long the water will look just like ink. So it is with sin.

Is it any wonder that so much trouble exists? But there is hope.

WHO CAN DESTROY
A STRONGHOLD?

No one! Not you! Not I! No human being can destroy a stronghold of Satan unless empowered by God. Even though we have personal responsibilities and there are many things we can and must do to thwart the powers of darkness, only God has the power to destroy strongholds. We may win a temporary victory by our own efforts, but only God will permanently prevail in spiritual warfare. Only with God's help can we live victoriously.

How many resolutions have I broken?

How many habits persist even after my all-out efforts to overcome them?

How many times have I failed in my limited and often feeble attempts to win the battle?

Even though the power of a stronghold may be temporarily restrained through human efforts, the stronghold itself still remains, patiently waiting to claim its victim. This is especially true with various addictions. The use of a substance may stop, but the desire or craving often continues.

Conversely, how many times have you known or heard about a person who was caught in a trap of one of the worst strongholds, but was totally and permanently freed when God moved in and took over? God, and God alone, is able.

If God fights the battle or empowers us with His weapons, the forces of evil cannot stand. They don't have a chance. The stronghold and all that goes with it is demolished. What once was is no more.

> *Greater is he that is in you, than he that is in the world.*   1 JOHN 4:4

While our own willpower and ability is never enough, God's grace and power never fails.

> *And he said unto me, My grace is sufficient for thee: for my strength is made perfect in weakness.*   2 CORINTHIANS 12:9

THE GREATEST STRONGHOLD

Often the thing that makes a stronghold more difficult is our inability to trust in God's ability to use our disability for His nobility—and for the love, care, and encouragement of others. In fact, the actual stronghold may not be as destructive as how we handle it! This might be our greatest stronghold!

Humbly, we need to realize that in God's big picture, and from an eternal perspective, His words are as true today as in the first century:

> *And we know that all things work together for good to them that love God, to them who are the called according to his purpose.*   ROMANS 8:28

As difficult as it is at times to understand, especially when everything is closing in and the circumstance is almost unbearable, God is able and does cause good to come from the worst of situations and conditions. If we are willing to allow Him to work His will, there will always be benefits derived from our suffering. We may not see them, or we may not be aware of them—yet.

Fact: If we cooperate, God uses our hard times

to equip us to be of comfort and encouragement to others. Only if I have experienced what you are experiencing—only if I've been there—can I honestly and sincerely say with compassion and empathy, "I know exactly how you feel."

> *Blessed be God, even the Father of our Lord*
> *Jesus Christ, the Father of mercies,*
> *and the God of all comfort;*
> *Who comforteth us in all our tribulation,*
> *that we may be able to comfort them which are*
> *in any trouble, by the comfort wherewith*
> *we ourselves are comforted of God.*
>
> 2 CORINTHIANS 1:3–4

Furthermore, our loving God may allow (not cause) our difficulties in order to help mold our character to become less self-reliant and more dependent on Him, and to help us develop an attitude of thanksgiving and appreciation for *all* things.

One of the great modern-day examples of a person God has used to bring comfort, encouragement, and inspiration to others through her own disability is Joni Eareckson Tada. Over thirty years ago, Joni suffered a broken neck in a diving accident that resulted in her becoming a quadriplegic at age seventeen.

During the years since, Joni has painted hundreds of beautiful pictures used in greeting cards by placing a pastel pencil between her teeth. She has a singing ministry, a speaking ministry, and a radio ministry. She heads her own organization, Joni and Friends, that, in addition to many other activities, works with churches and other facilities to make buildings handicap friendly. She has authored numerous books and magazine articles and is an inspiration to many thousands whose lives she has touched.

From her own testimony, one of Joni's greatest strongholds was her inability to trust in God's ability to use her disability for His nobility and for the love, care, and encouragement of others. But God changed all that. This courageous woman gained the unexpected victory! God has used her mightily.

He has made all things work together for good.

He has enabled Joni to encourage others by the same encouragement with which she herself has been encouraged by God!

Through His grace and power, what was once her stronghold has become her ministry.

This, my friend, is victory!

Joni Eareckson Tada is just one example of someone who found the secret to living in victory.

You can probably name many more yourself. In fact, one of them may be. . .or could be. . .you.

All of this does not mean that we should do nothing and adopt a defeatist attitude, saying, "I guess it's God's will for me to suffer so He can really use me." God wants us to be warriors. He wants us to be overcomers. He wants us to walk in the victory that Jesus won for us at Calvary. But at the same time, we must realize that often He does work in mysterious ways.

> *O the depth of the riches both of the wisdom and knowledge of God! how unsearchable are his judgments, and his ways past finding out!*
> ROMANS 11:33

Remember: Realizing the victory over strongholds is a process, not an event. It may take time, sometimes more than we are willing and seemingly able to give. We need to be reminded that a decade of years here on earth is but a mere blink of an eye in God's eternal spectrum of time.

> *But, beloved, be not ignorant of this one thing, that one day is with the Lord as a thousand years, and a thousand years as one day.*
> 2 PETER 3:8

God *is* in control and runs the scoreboard and the clock! There is a game to be played! A battle to be fought! A victory to be won! And He wants you in it.

Caution: As you prepare to gain this victory, be aware that changes will occur in your life. Perhaps for you the mere idea of change, even a desirable one, is a risk and something to be feared. For many, shedding the familiar (even though destructive and wrong) for the unfamiliar (new habits, new friendships) is just plain scary and a barrier to waging the battle.

Changes will occur, and indeed, they must occur, for you to gain the victory. But be assured, God is able, and will in time cause the unfamiliar to become familiar and the most desired.

If you have a problem anticipating the changes that will come about, you are not alone. Nearly everyone is somewhat fearful of the unknown. As you progress on your road to victory and pause to look back, you will be proud of your accomplishments and will be encouraged to continue on. God is with you.

PART II
THE BATTLE PLAN

STRATEGY AND TACTICS

Victory in any war is achieved one battle at a time. Although our war is not against flesh and blood but against the forces of Satan, it too must be fought one battle at a time. The outcome of our war—whether or not we live in victory—depends on the success or failure of many separate spiritual battles, and the destruction throughout a lifetime of many individual strongholds.

Just as in military wars, in order to be victorious a battle plan must be developed and followed.

The elements of our battle plan are as follows:

- Preparing to fight
- Receiving spiritual training
- Selecting weapons
- Waging the attack
- Establishing defenses (against the enemy's counterattacks)

Preparing to Fight

The first step can be summed up in just one sentence spoken by our Lord Jesus:

> *But seek ye first the kingdom of God, and his righteousness; and all these things shall be added unto you.*
> MATTHEW 6:33

These words are a small part of what has come to be known as the "Sermon on the Mount," in which Jesus described how the lives of people who have found the kingdom of God should be lived. Here He was emphasizing that we must not be concerned with daily cares, but that we should trust God for all our needs and continually seek the blessings of the kingdom. However, kingdom blessings, kingdom help, and kingdom victory can only be obtained by "subjects" of the King.

Do you want to live victoriously? Do you want to tear down the strongholds you are facing? If so, seek first the kingdom of God and His righteousness! This is where help is found. This is where victory can be won.

Jesus, in His wisdom and compassion, did not leave us clueless as to how we could find this kingdom. To Nicodemus, a brilliant Jewish scholar and ruler, He said, "Except a man be born again, he cannot see the kingdom of God" (John 3:3). Later, speaking to His disciple Thomas, Jesus defined His role:

Jesus saith unto him, I am the way, the truth, and the life: no man cometh unto the Father, but by me.   JOHN 14:6

When you come to the Father through Jesus—when you claim Jesus as your Lord and Savior, sincerely repent of your sins and ask His forgiveness, ask Him to come into your heart and take over your life, and commit your life to Him—your sins are forgiven and you receive spiritual life from God. Thus, you are born again and enter into the kingdom of God. When you came into this world, you were physically born of earthly parents. Now you are spiritually born from above. You are born of God. You are His child and a member of His family, and you are a citizen of His Kingdom.

Unless you have taken this step, you will continue to struggle and never be victorious. You are lacking the only power that can defeat the spiritual enemy—and that is the power of God.

If you have never made the decision to ask

Jesus into your heart and acted upon that decision, you may not be sure about Jesus. Among other things, you may be asking yourself, who is Jesus, and why did He come? Will He come again? You may also be wondering what it actually means to be born again, and how you can know for certain you have entered God's Kingdom. For help in dealing with these issues, you may want to skip ahead to the section entitled "Who Is Jesus?" (page 177) before continuing further.

But if you have taken the steps necessary to enter the kingdom of God, you are ready to avail yourself of God's power. You are ready to move on to the next step in preparing for battle.

RECEIVING
SPIRITUAL TRAINING

It is amazing to read how much time is spent on training and conditioning by those who aspire to be "the best." The best musicians or the best athletes or the tops in any field of endeavor weren't born great. They became great through countless hours (many of them painful) of training and conditioning. And even after they have arrived, so to speak, they continue to spend more time in training than they do in actual "combat."

And so it ought to be with the children of God. God's people need to be involved in the things of God, in spiritual training and spiritual exercises. The results? Spiritual growth and preparedness for battle.

Comparing your spiritual growth with physical growth, you didn't leave your mother's womb as a full-grown person but as an infant. And you didn't remain one for long! You received food and nourishment for your body and you grew to the stature you are today. The same is true of your spiritual person. You are not born spiritually mature. You grow spiritually because of the nutritional benefits of spiritual food and nourishment.

God has spiritual feasts prepared that are food

and nourishment to your soul. Although many seem to prefer to do so, you need not remain a spiritual babe. You will experience phenomenal spiritual growth when you partake of the food God offers.

> *As newborn babes, desire the sincere milk of the word, that ye may grow thereby.*   1 PETER 2:2

In understanding what is involved in your spiritual training program, realize that the kingdom of God is a personal relationship with God the Father, God the Son, and God the Holy Spirit. Your training and conditioning is designed to enhance that relationship. Spiritual growth is relational growth.

We must also remember, as Paul reminds us in an epistle, that the quest for spiritual growth and maturity is an ongoing process:

> *He which hath begun a good work in you will perform it until the day of Jesus Christ.*
> PHILIPPIANS 1:6

In other words, provided you are willing to continue training and to partake of the spiritual nutrition God has prepared, you will grow and mature spiritually until the day Jesus returns to this earth. That is when we all will reach spiritual maturity.

You also need to understand that even though it is the Holy Spirit who is doing the maturing work within you, your participation and cooperation are essential. What follows is a description of a few of the many things you can do to facilitate God's work.

DAILY DEVOTIONS

The Bible tells us that God created the world and all that is in it, including you and me, for His enjoyment and for us to enjoy Him.

> *Thou art worthy, O Lord, to receive glory and honour and power: for thou hast created all things, and for thy pleasure they are and were created.* REVELATION 4:11

As God's Word says, we were created for God's pleasure. Part of His pleasure is our pleasure in Him. How gratifying it must be to God when His children pay Him a visit! Just as our earthly parents are pleased by our attention to them, so is our heavenly Father, and even more so because

His love for us far surpasses any love a human being could give.

Our usual means of visiting with God is through prayer, Bible study, and meditation on His Word. Prayer is the means God has given each of us to speak to Him.

The Bible, the Living Word of God, is the principal means God uses to speak and to reveal Himself to us. When we study and meditate on His Word, we are given understanding by the Holy Spirit, who dwells within each child of God.

Without spending time with the Lord, it is virtually impossible to experience spiritual growth. But when you do reserve time for Him each day, it's amazing what happens to your relationship. With that in mind, consider making the "3 D's of Daily Devotion" an essential part of your life.

The first "D" is *desire*. If you will pray and ask God to give you the desire to spend part of each day (many prefer early morning) with Him, God will hear you and answer your prayer. After all, it is His desire, too. You may have to rise earlier than normal, but you'll be amazed at how the Lord will make it easy to forego that extra sleep. By the same token, God will provide time for you during the day or evening if that is your choice. In any event, set aside the same time each day, preferably in a place reserved for that purpose.

The second "D" is *discipline*. As before, if you will pray and ask God to give you the discipline necessary to visit with Him daily, He will again hear and answer your prayer.

Once you have prayed for desire and discipline and are engaged in daily devotions, you will never have to pray for the third "D." Your Father in heaven will be pleased to give you the delight that comes from being in His presence. The rewards are great! There is indescribable *delight*. That time will become very precious to you, and to God!

Lastly, when we come into the awesome, holy presence of the Lord, whether in daily devotion, worship or quiet time, or prayer, we want to do so thoroughly cleansed of sin. Listen to God's Word:

> *If I regard iniquity in my heart, the Lord will not hear me.*   PSALM 66:18

> *If we confess our sins, he is faithful and just to forgive us our sins, and to cleanse us from all unrighteousness.*   1 JOHN 1:9

Before beginning our time of prayer and study, we need to ask the Holy Spirit to reveal any sins we have committed, either knowingly or unknowingly, either sins of commission or sins of omission, and then confess those specific sins and seek God's forgiveness.

FASTING

Literally hundreds of volumes have been written and many sermons preached on the discipline of fasting. It would be impossible to cover this subject thoroughly in just a few paragraphs. However, several observations about fasting as it relates to spiritual growth are important.

Among the sixty-plus examples of fasting mentioned in the Bible, by far the most important is Jesus' fast for forty days in preparation for His temptation by Satan, prior to the beginning of His ministry (see Matthew 4:1–11). The practice of fasting, as demonstrated by Jesus, is a means of enjoying and drawing closer to God and an important element in spiritual training and growth. While there are many ways to fast other than giving up food and drink, our discussion will be limited to that type of fast.

Food and drink is a gift and a blessing from God. The problem is, do we prefer God's gifts and blessings more than we prefer Him? When we fast, we demonstrate our preference for God Himself. Our focus is on Him, our relationship with Him, and our spiritual needs, not on the needs of the body.

Here are several additional thoughts concerning fasting:

- My concentration is on God, not on the fast. The purpose is to focus on Him, not on the "great sacrifice" I am making or what I am giving up.

- Fasting is a private matter between God and me. To the degree possible, it's not necessary to let other people know what I am doing.

- During a fast, I need to spend as much time as possible in praise and worship and prayer and Bible study.

- Spiritually, I ought to prepare for a fast at least several days in advance. Much time should be spent in prayer.

- It is desirable to prepare physically for a fast, especially a long one. Information concerning this may be obtained at a health food store. Also, consult a physician regarding any known medical condition that might be diet sensitive.

- If I have a specific purpose for fasting, I should be certain it is in the will of God.

This exercise of putting God before the needs of the body—putting God before self—will always result in a closer walk with Him, provided the motivation is right. (For a more in-depth study of fasting, I recommend the book *A Hunger for God* by John Piper [Crossway Books, 1997].)

GATHERING TOGETHER

The Bible tells us that we should "not [be] forsaking the assembling of ourselves together" (Hebrews 10:25). We cannot stress too strongly the importance of people of like mind and purpose meeting together for praise and worship, fellowship with each other, and to receive guidance and instruction in the things of God.

One of the reasons for assembling or gathering together is to be obedient to God's "one another" commands. There are over fifty passages in the Bible pertaining to the relationship between brothers and sisters in Christ. Among them are:

- Love one another (John 13:34).
- Serve one another (Galatians 5:13).
- Submit to one another (Ephesians 5:21).
- Forgive one another (Colossians 3:13).
- Pray for one another (James 5:16).

It's difficult to be obedient to these commands when we don't know the person we are trying to love, serve, submit to, forgive, pray for, and encourage. We get to know people by being with people. We get to know them by gathering together.

Another reason to meet with other Christians is to fellowship corporately with Christ. Jesus tells us, "For where two or three are gathered together in my name, there am I in the midst of them" (Matthew 18:20). Based on His own words, not only is Jesus with us when we meet with Him in groups of two or three, but when we meet as a church body in His name. He enjoys our fellowship and we His.

There are many who do not attend church in order to engage in other activities. Most of us have heard someone say, "I can worship God just as well without being in church. I can find God in nature." This may be possible but is obviously questionable. The Sunday morning golfer, the weekend fisherman, and the sports enthusiast may be enjoying nature and the great outdoors and "fellowshipping" with others, but are they really in touch with God? I've never heard of many prayers being offered, or praises sung, or Bible passages meditated upon by a person trying to hit the perfect drive or land the big one. It all sounds good, but it just doesn't happen.

Your spiritual growth will be greatly enhanced by your personal involvement in a Christ-centered and Bible-teaching church. Sad to say, however, there are many that are not offering spiritual nourishment but rather are offering worldly junk food. Ask God to direct you to a place where His food is offered, and where His presence is known. Only in such a place will you receive the nourishment you require.

FORGIVING OTHERS

One of the greatest deterrents to a mature spiritual life is a spirit of bitterness and unforgiveness. Such an attitude has probably done as much to stunt spiritual growth as anything we can name, and yet it is so common, even among the children of God. We fail to realize the seriousness of this sin in the eyes of God.

And be ye kind one to another, tenderhearted, forgiving one another, even as God for Christ's sake hath forgiven you. EPHESIANS 4:32

[Jesus said,]For if ye forgive men their trespasses, your heavenly Father will also forgive you: But if ye forgive not men their trespasses, neither will your Father forgive your trespasses. MATTHEW 6:14–15

These are not idle words. Forgiving others is what God expects and requires of us. He is fully aware of the damage bitterness and lack of forgiveness can do, not only to the relationships between brothers and sisters in Christ but to His kingdom. He just doesn't permit it.

If I can ever comprehend how much I have to be forgiven for, the enormity of God's unconditional forgiveness, and how great the sacrifice He made on the cross for me, I would be more than ready to forgive others who have harmed me.

Do you believe we sin, either intentionally or

unintentionally, at least several times a day? Let's say we sin twice a day. That means in ten years we will have committed over seven thousand sins, and in thirty years nearly twenty-two thousand, and that's just for starters. Our disobedience to God, in thought, word, and deed, occurs many times more than twice a day. When we consider that just one sin qualifies us for eternal punishment, then God's capacity to forgive becomes even more amazing—and ours should be just like His.

We have a God who loves us so much that He is not bitter toward us for the ways in which we have disobeyed and wronged Him. How pleased He must be when we exhibit that same spirit toward others!

For you, forgiving may be extremely difficult. You may have had things done to you that in human terms seem impossible to forgive. But God says if you or I don't forgive others, regardless of the magnitude of the wrong against us or how deeply we may have been hurt, He will not forgive us. What is the answer?

It just makes sense that if you are not able to forgive and God is, why not just turn it over to Him? Release it, let it go, and let God take care of it.

A sincere prayer such as the one that follows

not only relieves you of the responsibility of forgiving, but is in itself an act of forgiveness. What a blessing and what relief!

> *Heavenly Father,*
> *I have carried this burden far too long. It eats*
> *and eats at me. My lack of forgiveness and my*
> *bitterness has become a barrier between You and*
> *me. I now release this matter to You. It is in*
> *Your hands. I am freed from it. Thank You,*
> *Lord.*

Asking the one who harmed you (the one who is at fault) for their forgiveness is also a spiritually enriching way to forgive, as I know firsthand. Some time ago a close friend seriously wronged me in a business matter. After hearing an excellent sermon on forgiveness, and being convicted by it, I went to my friend and repeated the words the pastor had suggested: "I've come here today to ask your forgiveness. Since our misunderstanding, I have been angry with you and have had bitterness in my heart toward you. Will you please forgive me?"

Immediately the burden was lifted and the relationship was renewed. Notice, though, that the wrong my friend had committed was not mentioned, nor was my forgiveness of him. These things were no longer an issue. My act of asking him for his forgiveness was also an act of forgiving him, and the wounds were healed.

Why should I ask his forgiveness? you may wonder. After all, he's the one who hurt me. The answer is as simple as the question is obvious. In order for any strained relationship to be healed, someone has to go first! You'll be amazed at the blessings you will receive when you're the one who makes the first move.

Another way to plant the seed of forgiveness in your own heart, and then to watch it grow, is to pray for the person who has harmed you. This too may be difficult, but it is what the Lord has asked us to do. Again, hear Jesus' words from the Sermon on the Mount:

> *But I say unto you, Love your enemies, bless them that curse you, do good to them that hate you, and pray for them which despitefully use you, and persecute you.* MATTHEW 5:44

We must be careful how we pray for the one who has "done us wrong." Any such prayer should come out of genuine compassion and concern. It's very easy to fall into the "Pharisee trap" and exalt ourselves while we belittle the other person, using prayer as the instrument. Among other things, we need to sincerely pray for a person's salvation and spiritual prosperity; that their needs be met; and that God would pour out His grace upon them.

QUESTION: Is it possible that my lack of forgiveness not only is a barrier between God and me, but somehow is also affecting that person's relationship with God? If this could possibly be, it would seem there is double jeopardy on my part.

Be aware! Often when we forgive someone, we do so with the expectation that they will change completely as a person. The effects of our act of forgiveness on the person may be great enough to foster change, but we also may be letting ourselves in for considerable disappointment. Our purpose in forgiving is not to change human nature, but to cleanse our heart and heal relationships.

Developing a forgiving heart and a heart free from bitterness toward others will go a long way in preparing you for spiritual battle.

Controlling Thoughts

Finally, brethren, whatsoever things are true,
whatsoever things are honest, whatsoever
things are just, whatsoever things are pure,
whatsoever things are lovely, whatsoever
things are of good report; if there be any virtue,
and if there be any praise, think on these
things.   Philippians 4:8

When the apostle Paul wrote these words to the church at Philippi, he did so knowing full well the beneficial effects of right thinking and the destructive effects of harmful thoughts. Since Paul's time, there probably have been as many books written on this subject as any other. This section is not meant as an explanation or endorsement of worldly "positive thinking" or the "name it and claim it" philosophy, but as an encouragement for all of us to be engaged in godly thinking.

Many thoughts are barriers to spiritual growth and our relationship with God. The person in training for spiritual battle will do well to be continually aware of destructive thoughts and immediately take measures to substitute spiritually enriching ones. Here are a few measures we can consider:

• "Commit thy works unto the LORD, and thy

thoughts shall be established" (Proverbs 16:3).

- Make God the center of our attention, and pure thoughts will be the rule.
- Substitute favorite Scripture for damaging thoughts.
- Memorize a number of short passages from the Bible that have encouraged you, and repeat one of them aloud when you find yourself thinking harmful thoughts.
- Pray for someone else, one of the most effective means of thought management.

Think about it. How many people do you know who need your prayers at this very moment or at any other moment? When a wrong thought enters your mind, immediately, without hesitation, begin to pray for someone. It's amazing how quickly the damaging thought is replaced with those the apostle Paul described.

ACTS OF CARE
AND ENCOURAGEMENT

A proven way to grow spiritually and get your mind off your own problems is to care enough to daily do something that will be of encouragement to another person.

We often get so wrapped up in our own circumstances that we fail to see the unlimited opportunities we have to encourage others. And the truth is that the encouragement that is most appreciated and most effective comes from someone who is experiencing difficulties themselves—someone who has their own strongholds to overcome.

This world is full of hurting people who need your smile, visit, telephone call, letter, and prayers. The encouragement you bring to others, and the spiritual blessings, will always be returned to you many times over. Guaranteed!

GIVING THANKS

What amazing grace God exhibits by continuing to shower us with blessings, even when we so often fail to thank Him for those we have already received!

Yes, everything we have, from the most important to the least important, comes from God. Regardless of how many difficulties we might be experiencing, when we consider all that we do have, our gratitude ought to be constantly expressed.

Just as everyone appreciates receiving thanks for things they do, God appreciates our thanks for what He has done, is doing, and will do. In many Bible passages, we are encouraged to give thanks. In fact, God even considers it to be a type of sacrifice on our part.

I will offer to thee the sacrifice of thanksgiving, and will call upon the name of the LORD.

PSALM 116:17

It is often difficult to be grateful when we are beset with what might appear to be insurmountable problems. Yet the Bible is clear:

In every thing give thanks: for this is the will of God in Christ Jesus concerning you.

1 THESSALONIANS 5:18

Every person has many reasons to be thankful: for life. . .God. . .family. . .church. . .food. . . home. . .pets. . .clothes. . .job. . .and on and on. There is no end to the list of things both material and spiritual that God has provided for each of us.

Here's a suggestion: During your daily devotions, write down several things that you are thankful for, and give God thanks for them. Keep the list in your Bible, and add several new things each day. Thank God for even the smallest thing you can imagine. Nothing is too insignificant!

The list I keep now has several hundred items on it. Many of them, like the orange juice I have in the morning, or the pen I'm using, or the shoes I'm wearing, may seem trivial, but they came from God, and I want to thank Him for them. As I look back over the list occasionally, my appreciation of what a wonderful God I have grows—and you are sure to feel the same.

DAILY DEVOTIONS
FASTING
GATHERING TOGETHER
FORGIVING OTHERS
CONTROLLING THOUGHTS
ACTS OF CARE AND ENCOURAGEMENT
GIVING THANKS

These are but a few of the many disciplines we can utilize in our spiritual training. Remember: Proficiency in any endeavor is never accomplished in one fell swoop. Training is always conducted one step or one phase at a time. For some, considering all the disciplines available for spiritual training may even be overwhelming but it need not be. Begin your training with just one discipline and add the others as the Lord leads you. He knows better than you when you are ready for the next step.

SELECTING THE WEAPONS

PRAISE AND WORSHIP

*I will call on the LORD, who is worthy to be
praised: so shall I be saved from mine enemies.*
2 SAMUEL 22:4

*Oh that men would praise the LORD for his
goodness, and for his wonderful works to the
children of men!* PSALM 107:8

Whoso offereth praise glorifieth me.
PSALM 50:23

*Let every thing that hath breath praise the
LORD. Praise ye the LORD.* PSALM 150:6

Every day we ought to praise and worship God
continually. Every time of devotion needs to be
preceded by praise and worship. Every church
service should begin with praise and worship.
God is more than deserving, and His heart is
warmed by our efforts. God's power is manifested
in a new and mighty way through praise and worship, and your life will be changed through your
participation. Praise and worship glorifies God
and prepares the way for the use of the other

weapons God has provided for us, weapons to tear down the strongholds that stand in the way of living victoriously. Praise and worship, our first mighty weapon, should always be followed by prayer.

PRAYER

If we can ever fully comprehend the power of prayer and the wonderful privilege God has granted in permitting us to communicate directly with Him in this manner, we will be truly humbled. Here is Almighty God, who is absolutely holy and absolutely perfect, who created the universe and owns all that is in it, welcoming us into His presence when we pray. And the best part is, He never fails to answer! He may not always give us what we think we want, but He always answers—in His timing.

The Bible speaks often concerning the privilege of prayer.

> *Let us therefore come boldly unto the throne of grace, that we may obtain mercy, and find grace to help in time of need.* HEBREWS 4:16

The sacrifice of the wicked is an abomination to the LORD: but the prayer of the upright is his delight.   PROVERBS 15:8

The effectual fervent prayer of a righteous man availeth much.   JAMES 5:16

Evening, and morning, and at noon, will I pray, and cry aloud: and he shall hear my voice.
                    PSALM 55:17

Pray without ceasing.   1 THESSALONIANS 5:17

There are many additional passages that not only encourage us to spend much time in prayer, but tell of God's willingness to hear—and answer. Someone once said, "Nothing happens until someone prays!" The truth of this as it relates to spiritual warfare is of the utmost importance. Without sufficient time in prayer, we fail to utilize a powerful weapon, and nothing happens. Indeed, "Nothing happens until *we* pray."

THE WORD OF GOD

And take the helmet of salvation, and the sword of the Spirit, which is the word of God.

EPHESIANS 6:17

This powerful Scripture describes our next offensive weapon, the Word of God! In this passage, Paul is describing some of the weapons God provides us with to protect ourselves against the devil.

The Word of God is a weapon of the Holy Spirit, who empowers us to use it.

The Word of God is the sword of the Spirit, and as such, the Bible is both an offensive and a defensive weapon. First, Satan cannot defend himself against the Word of God. And we can use passages from the Bible as weapons to attack and defeat the enemy.

Fear thou not; for I am with thee: be not dismayed; for I am thy God: I will strengthen thee; yea, I will help thee; yea, I will uphold thee with the right hand of my righteousness. . . . For I the LORD thy God will hold thy right hand, saying unto thee, Fear not; I will help thee.

ISAIAH 41:10, 13

This Scripture is one of hundreds that can be

used as "weapons" in your quest for victory. Indeed, the Bible is filled with God's promises to fight for us and with us. As I repeat these words aloud, I can feel God strengthening me and upholding me with His right hand of righteousness. I can feel my hand in His as He guides and helps me. God gives me the assurance that no force of evil can affect me when I am under His protection.

THE NAME OF JESUS

And whatsoever ye shall ask in my name, that will I do, that the Father may be glorified in the Son.

If ye shall ask any thing in my name, I will do it. JOHN 14:13–14

If there is anything Satan detests and cowers from, it is the name of Jesus.

Jesus has given all believers in Him the authority to use His name in defeating the works of Satan and his demons.

A well-known example of the use of the name of Jesus is found in the Book of Acts. Peter and John were going to the temple for prayer when they passed a beggar who had been crippled from birth. When the poor man asked the apostles for money, Peter said:

> *Silver and gold have I none; but such as I have give I thee: In the name of Jesus Christ of Nazareth rise up and walk.* ACTS 3:6

The man was instantly healed and, walking and leaping and praising God, he joined Peter and John in the temple. Later, when Peter spoke concerning this miracle to the crowd that had gathered, he said "And his name through faith in his name hath made this man strong" (Acts 3:16).

Yes, Jesus graciously permits and encourages us to use His name reverently in the destruction of strongholds.

THE BLOOD OF THE LAMB

> *And they overcame him by the blood of the Lamb, and by the word of their testimony.* REVELATION 12:11

When Jesus died on the cross and shed His blood for the unconditional forgiveness of sins for all those who would accept His sacrifice and follow

Him, He became God's very own sacrificial lamb. Thus, when we speak of "overcoming by the blood of the Lamb," we speak of the power of the blood of Jesus Christ shed for the sins of the world.

Among the many treasures that speak of the blood of Christ is the old hymn "There Is Power in the Blood" written by Lewis Ellis Jones in 1899. The first verse and chorus are as follows:

> *Would you be free from the burden of sin?*
> *There's power in the blood, power in the blood.*
> *Would you over evil a victory win?*
> *There's wonderful power in the blood.*

> *There is power, power, wonder-working power*
> *in the blood of the Lamb.*
> *There is power, power, wonder working power*
> *in the precious blood of the Lamb.*

Total, everlasting victory over Satan was won at Calvary by the blood of Christ and His resurrection. The power of the blood still prevails, and children of God have the privilege and right to plead the blood of the Lamb for protection for ourselves and those we care about. Such earnest requests include for healing, the destruction of strongholds, and for the defeat of Satan.

Pleading the blood is not commonly practiced in today's Christian climate, but the "old-timers" knew the cleansing, healing, protecting, renewing, purifying, and perfecting power of the blood of the Lamb, and they used it often against the devil. It was and still is a major weapon in our spiritual warfare. (Note: Many examples of miracles wrought by pleading the blood have been recorded. *The Blood and the Glory* by Billye Brim [Harrison House, 1995] is an excellent source of information on this subject.)

PRAISE AND WORSHIP
PRAYER
THE WORD OF GOD
THE NAME OF JESUS
THE BLOOD OF THE LAMB

God has empowered us to use these "weapons of spiritual warfare" for His glory and our victory. Let us begin!

WAGING THE ATTACK

It is not likely that we would use all of our weapons simultaneously in waging our attack. We may want to use a combination of several weapons, or even just one. You may use different combinations at different times. What is important is becoming proficient in the use of each weapon. What you will learn here is a suggested way to put each weapon to work for you.

When weapons are used is important. While you will most often use them at a special time, like during daily devotions, as you begin to see results and as you gain confidence in the eventual victory, you will find that during each day, and even during the night, you will be led by the Holy Spirit to engage in battle. The battle can be fought anytime, anywhere.

Above all, we must guard against the use of weapons becoming a routine that is mechanically repeated over and over. We ought to engage in each attack with renewed vigor and confidence.

Our assault begins with our first weapon: praise and worship.

During praise and worship:

- Spend time audibly thanking God for all

that He does and praising Him for who He is and His love for you.

- Pray psalms of praise aloud.
- Sing songs of praise aloud.
- Lift your heart and hands to God in praise. (See Psalms 25:1; 28:2; 63:4; 1 Kings 8:54; Nehemiah 8:6; Lamentations 3:41; and 1 Timothy 2:8.)
- Release your feelings and emotions to God. Let your love flow to Him. Praise Him! Worship Him! Adore Him! Exalt Him! Bless Him! Tell Him!

Our attack continues with the powerful weapon of prayer, which launches the remaining three weapons. The following are suggested prayers, given under headings that indicate their particular focus.

THE WORD

Heavenly Father,
I believe in the power of Your Word. I believe it is the sword of the Spirit, and I call upon it now in the destruction of the stronghold of
_____ *in my life.*

Attack with the Word by reading aloud, or repeating aloud from memory, passages of Scripture that encourage you and speak to the stronghold in your life. You may feel the need to repeat these Scriptures a number of times during the day. If you desire, turn to the section entitled "The Sword of the Spirit" (page 69), which contains numerous prayerfully selected passages of Scripture.

THE NAME

In the name of Jesus, I take control of the stronghold of _____ in my life. I plead the power of the name of Jesus in the destruction of this stronghold.

THE BLOOD

Dear Lord,
I agree to the power of the blood of the Lamb, and I now plead the cleansing, healing, protecting, renewing, purifying, and perfecting power of this blood over the stronghold of _____.
Remove it, Lord. Deliver me from it.

THE PRAYER OF THANKSGIVING

Lord God,
I thank You for the power of Your weapons that
are defeating Satan and destroying the strong-
hold of _____ in my life. I thank
You for the strength You are giving me, for Your
love, for Your amazing grace, Your mercy, and
the victory we are gaining.

Pray aloud. Pray confidently and expectantly. God is empowering you. He is fighting with you and for you. You are on the winning team—and on your way to living in victory.

ESTABLISHING DEFENSES

When victory over a particular stronghold has been achieved, we cannot afford to become complacent. We are still subject to attack, though perhaps in a different way, but always from the same enemy.

For those who have never accepted Christ as their Savior, or are not engaged in the disciplines we have previously discussed, a subtle means of attack that Satan often employs is a feeling of loss or emptiness. As is especially true with smoking and other similar habits, despite how destructive the habit might have been, it's almost like losing a friend. We have relied upon certain habits for so long, and they have become such a part of our lives, that their absence is felt. But, praise God, if we are persistent in our spiritual training, and if we are diligent in the use of our weapons, the Holy Spirit fills the void that might normally exist.

Let's turn again to the Book of Ephesians where Paul names what constitutes the "whole armour of God." This armor is provided by God so that we will be "able to withstand in the evil day, and having done all, to stand" (Ephesians 6:13).

We are to wear the belt of truth and the "breastplate of righteousness"; have our "feet shod with the preparation of the gospel of peace"; put on "the shield of faith" and "the helmet of salvation"; and take and use "the sword of the Spirit, which is the word of God." (See Ephesians 6:14–17.)

These are defensive weapons that we must wear daily to thwart the attacks of Satan. Each morning we can visualize ourselves putting on this armor to prepare for the day. This is God's own armor that He empowers us to use.

In addition, we have all heard the saying, "The best defense is a good offense." If we are practicing daily devotions; fasting; gathering together; forgiving others; controlling thoughts; acts of care and encouragement; and giving thanks, and if we are using the weapons of praise and worship; prayer; the Word of God; the name of Jesus; and the blood of the Lamb, we are continually and consistently on the offensive against the person and works of Satan. Our offense is our best defense. Satan is thwarted. We will be strong in the Lord and the power of His might.

IN CONCLUSION

To live in victory is never easy. Success can come only through great effort and persistence. If you are willing to give this effort, and if you are willing to trust fully in God for His guidance and His strength, victory will be yours.

We live in a country of instant gratification. We look for quick solutions. We are impatient people who live for today. Our prayer often goes, "Lord, give me patience and do it now!" We expect God to destroy strongholds in a day that may have taken months or even years to build.

He may or He may not act immediately, but He will respond. However, His response will always be in His timing. We need to persevere with our spiritual training and with our use of spiritual weapons, and then leave the rest up to God. We need to wait on the Lord—expectantly.

Wait on the LORD: be of good courage, and he shall strengthen thine heart: wait, I say, on the LORD. PSALM 27:14

Cast not away therefore your confidence, which hath great recompense of reward. For ye have need of patience, that, after ye have done the will of God, ye might receive the promise. HEBREWS 10:35–36

PART III
THE SWORD OF THE SPIRIT
(THE WORD OF GOD)

A POWERFUL WEAPON

On the following pages, you will find passages of Scripture that may be used as weapons in your march to victory. You may also want to explore your Bible for your own selections. Here are several suggestions concerning their use:

- Read the Scriptures aloud if possible. ("So then faith cometh by hearing, and hearing by the word of God" [Romans 10:17].)
- Select those Scriptures that seem to speak most to your needs and have special meaning for you.
- Write your selections on three-by-five-inch cards, and carry them with you at all times. Read aloud or repeat aloud from memory as often as needed during each day.
- Memorize at least one selection each week.
- Become familiar with as many Scriptures as possible in this section. Read the Scripture in its original context in your Bible. You will find that what goes before and follows will often give even greater meaning to your selection.

GETTING STARTED

The next several pages may be used to write descriptions of any strongholds in your life and scriptural "weapons" you may choose.

STRONGHOLD DESCRIPTION:
(Write a description of any stronghold in your life.)

_____

_____

_____

_____

_____

_____

_____

_____

_____

_____

_____

_____

_____

My Sword of the Spirit:
(Write passages of Scripture you will use as your sword of the Spirit.)

_____

_____

_____

_____

_____

_____

_____

_____

_____

_____

_____

_____

_____

_____

_____

_____

_____

_____

_____

_____

_____

_____

_____

_____

_____

_____

_____

STRONGHOLD DESCRIPTION:
(Write a description of any stronghold in your life.)

_____

_____

_____

_____

_____

_____

_____

_____

_____

My Sword of the Spirit:
(Write passages of Scripture you will use as your sword of the Spirit.)

_____

_____

_____

_____

_____

_____

_____

_____

_____

_____

_____

_____

_____

_____

_____

_____

_____

_____

_____

_____

_____

_____

_____

_____

_____

_____

_____

_____

_____

_____

_____

_____

_____

_____

_____

_____

_____

_____

_____

_____

_____

_____

_____

_____

STRONGHOLD DESCRIPTION:
(Write a description of any stronghold in your life.)

_____

_____

_____

_____

_____

_____

_____

_____

_____

_____

_____

_____

_____

_____

_____

_____

_____

_____

_____

MY SWORD OF THE SPIRIT:
(Write passages of Scripture you will use as your sword of the Spirit.)

_____

_____

_____

_____

_____

_____

_____

_____

_____

_____

_____

_____

_____

_____

_____

_____

_____

THE SWORD OF THE SPIRIT

All Scripture is from the King James Version of the Bible. (Note: Where words in the original text might be misconstrued or not understood, an explanatory word or phrase is provided inside brackets within the Scripture.) To aid in your devotions, Scripture has been divided into several topical categories.

YOU CAN RELY
UPON GOD'S WORD

It is the spirit that quickeneth; the flesh profiteth nothing: the words that I speak unto you, they are spirit, and they are life.   JOHN 6:63

For my thoughts are not your thoughts, neither are your ways my ways, saith the LORD.

For as the heavens are higher than the earth, so are my ways higher than your ways, and my thoughts than your thoughts.

For as the rain cometh down, and the snow from heaven, and returneth not thither, but watereth the earth, and maketh it bring forth

and bud, that it may give seed to the sower, and
bread to the eater:
  So shall my word be that goeth forth out of
my mouth: it shall not return unto me void, but
it shall accomplish that which I please, and it
shall prosper in the thing whereto I sent it.
                                              Isaiah 55:8–11

Thy word is a lamp unto my feet, and a light
unto my path.   Psalm 119:105

The entrance of thy words giveth light; it giveth
understanding unto the simple.   Psalm 119:130

Thy word have I hid in mine heart, that I
might not sin against thee.   Psalm 119:11

For ever, O Lord, thy word is settled in heaven.
  Thy faithfulness is unto all generations:
thou hast established the earth, and it abideth.
                                              Psalm 119:89–90

We have also a more sure word of prophecy;
whereunto ye do well that ye take heed, as unto
a light that shineth in a dark place, until the
day dawn, and the day star arise in your hearts:
  Knowing this first, that no prophecy of the
scripture is of any private interpretation.
  For the prophecy came not in old time by

the will of man: but holy men of God spake as they were moved by the Holy Ghost.

2 PETER 1:19–21

Yea, and all that will live godly in Christ Jesus shall suffer persecution.

But evil men and seducers shall wax worse and worse, deceiving, and being deceived.

But continue thou in the things which thou hast learned and hast been assured of, knowing of whom thou hast learned them;

And that from a child thou hast known the holy scriptures, which are able to make thee wise unto salvation through faith which is in Christ Jesus.

All scripture is given by inspiration of God, and is profitable for doctrine, for reproof, for correction, for instruction in righteousness:

That the man of God may be perfect, thoroughly furnished unto all good works.

2 TIMOTHY 3:12–17

The grass withereth, the flower fadeth: but the word of our God shall stand for ever.

ISAIAH 40:8

For this cause also thank we God without ceasing, because, when ye received the word of God which ye heard of us, ye received it not as the word of men, but as it is in truth, the word of God, which effectually worketh also in you that believe.   1 THESSALONIANS 2:13

Heaven and earth shall pass away: but my words shall not pass away.   LUKE 21:33

For the oppression of the poor, for the sighing of the needy, now will I arise, saith the LORD; I will set him in safety from him that puffeth at him.

The words of the LORD are pure words: as silver tried in a furnace of earth, purified seven times.   PSALM 12:5–6

For the word of God is quick, and powerful, and sharper than any twoedged sword, piercing even to the dividing asunder of soul and spirit, and of the joints and marrow, and is a discerner of the thoughts and intents of the heart.

HEBREWS 4:12

GOD IS AWESOME

Then he answered and spake unto me, saying,
This is the word of the LORD unto Zerubbabel,
saying, Not by might, nor by power, but by my
spirit, saith the LORD of hosts.   ZECHARIAH 4:6

Heal me, O LORD, and I shall be healed; save
me, and I shall be saved: for thou art my praise.
                                    JEREMIAH 17:14

Make a joyful noise unto the LORD, all ye lands.
    Serve the LORD with gladness: come before
his presence with singing.
    Know ye that the LORD he is God: it is he
that hath made us, and not we ourselves; we are
his people, and the sheep of his pasture.
    Enter into his gates with thanksgiving, and
into his courts with praise: be thankful unto
him, and bless his name.
    For the LORD is good; his mercy is everlast-
ing; and his truth endureth to all generations.
                                    PSALM 100

But ye are a chosen generation, a royal priest-
hood, an holy nation, a peculiar people; that ye
should shew forth the praises of him who hath
called you out of darkness into his marvellous
light.   1 PETER 2:9

We have heard with our ears, O God, our fathers have told us, what work thou didst in their days, in the times of old.

How thou didst drive out the heathen with thy hand, and plantedst them; how thou didst afflict the people, and cast them out.

For they got not the land in possession by their own sword, neither did their own arm save them: but thy right hand, and thine arm, and the light of thy countenance, because thou hadst a favour unto them. PSALM 44:1–3

I will sing of the mercies of the LORD for ever: with my mouth will I make known thy faithfulness to all generations. PSALM 89:1

The heavens declare the glory of God; and the firmament sheweth his handywork.

Day unto day uttereth speech, and night unto night sheweth knowledge.

There is no speech nor language, where their voice is not heard. PSALM 19:1–3

With the merciful thou wilt shew thyself merciful, and with the upright man thou wilt shew thyself upright.

With the pure thou wilt shew thyself pure; and with the froward thou wilt shew thyself unsavoury.

And the afflicted people thou wilt save: but thine eyes are upon the haughty, that thou mayest bring them down.

For thou art my lamp, O LORD: and the LORD will lighten my darkness.

For by thee I have run through a troop: by my God have I leaped over a wall.

2 SAMUEL 22:26–30

If it had not been the LORD who was on our side, now may Israel say;

If it had not been the LORD who was on our side, when men rose up against us:

Then they had swallowed us up quick, when their wrath was kindled against us:

Then the waters had overwhelmed us, the stream had gone over our soul:

Then the proud waters had gone over our soul.

Blessed be the LORD, who hath not given us as a prey to their teeth.

Our soul is escaped as a bird out of the snare of the fowlers: the snare is broken, and we are escaped.

Our help is in the name of the LORD, who made heaven and earth.

PSALM 124

Hast thou not known? hast thou not heard, that the everlasting God, the LORD, the Creator of the ends of the earth, fainteth not, neither is weary? there is no searching of his understanding.

He giveth power to the faint; and to them that have no might he increaseth strength.

Even the youths shall faint and be weary, and the young men shall utterly fall:

But they that wait upon the LORD shall renew their strength; they shall mount up with wings as eagles; they shall run, and not be weary; and they shall walk, and not faint.

ISAIAH 40:28–31

For thou hast possessed my reins: thou hast covered me in my mother's womb.

I will praise thee; for I am fearfully and wonderfully made: marvellous are thy works; and that my soul knoweth right well.

My substance was not hid from thee, when I was made in secret, and curiously wrought in the lowest parts of the earth.

Thine eyes did see my substance, yet being unperfect; and in thy book all my members were written, which in continuance were fashioned, when as yet there was none of them.

How precious also are thy thoughts unto me, O God! how great is the sum of them!

If I should count them, they are more in number than the sand: when I awake, I am still with thee.

PSALM 139:13–18

God is not a man, that he should lie; neither the son of man, that he should repent: hath he said, and shall he not do it? or hath he spoken, and shall he not make it good? NUMBERS 23:19

They that go down to the sea in ships, that do business in great waters;

These see the works of the LORD, and his wonders in the deep.

For he commandeth, and raiseth the stormy wind, which lifteth up the waves thereof.

They mount up to the heaven, they go down again to the depths: their soul is melted because of trouble.

They reel to and fro, and stagger like a drunken man, and are at their wit's end.

Then they cry unto the LORD in their trouble, and he bringeth them out of their distresses.

He maketh the storm a calm, so that the waves thereof are still.

Then are they glad because they be quiet; so he bringeth them unto their desired haven.

Oh that men would praise the LORD for his goodness, and for his wonderful works to the children of men!

Let them exalt him also in the congregation of the people, and praise him in the assembly of the elders. PSALM 107:23–32

Praise ye the LORD. Praise, O ye servants of the LORD, praise the name of the LORD.

Blessed be the name of the LORD from this time forth and for evermore.

From the rising of the sun unto the going down of the same the LORD's name is to be praised.

The LORD is high above all nations, and his glory above the heavens.

Who is like unto the LORD our God, who dwelleth on high,

Who humbleth himself to behold the things that are in heaven, and in the earth!

He raiseth up the poor out of the dust, and lifteth the needy out of the dunghill;

That he may set him with princes, even with the princes of his people.

He maketh the barren woman to keep house, and to be a joyful mother of children. Praise ye the LORD.   PSALM 113

I will be glad and rejoice in thee: I will sing praise to thy name, O thou most High.

When mine enemies are turned back, they shall fall and perish at thy presence.

For thou hast maintained my right and my cause; thou satest in the throne judging right.

                                        PSALM 9:2–4

I know that, whatsoever God doeth, it shall be for ever: nothing can be put to it, nor any thing taken from it: and God doeth it, that men should fear before him. ECCLESIASTES 3:14

Blessed be the LORD God, the God of Israel, who only doeth wondrous things. PSALM 72:18

Thy mercy, O LORD, is in the heavens; and thy faithfulness reacheth unto the clouds.

Thy righteousness is like the great mountains; thy judgments are a great deep: O LORD, thou preservest man and beast.

How excellent is thy lovingkindness, O God! therefore the children of men put their trust under the shadow of thy wings.

They shall be abundantly satisfied with the fatness of thy house; and thou shalt make them drink of the river of thy pleasures.

For with thee is the fountain of life: in thy light shall we see light.

O continue thy lovingkindness unto them that know thee; and thy righteousness to the upright in heart. PSALM 36:5–10

Behold, God is my salvation; I will trust, and not be afraid: for the LORD JEHOVAH is my strength and my song; he also is become my salvation. ISAIAH 12:2

For it is God which worketh in you both to will and to do of his good pleasure.   PHILIPPIANS 2:13

Many, O LORD my God, are thy wonderful works which thou hast done, and thy thoughts which are to us-ward: they cannot be reckoned up in order unto thee: if I would declare and speak of them, they are more than can be numbered.
PSALM 40:5

The silver is mine, and the gold is mine, saith the LORD of hosts.   HAGGAI 2:8

Be still, and know that I am God: I will be exalted among the heathen, I will be exalted in the earth.
The LORD of hosts is with us; the God of Jacob is our refuge. Selah.   PSALM 46:10–11

For the earth shall be filled with the knowledge of the glory of the LORD, as the waters cover the sea.
HABAKKUK 2:14

Rejoice in the Lord alway: and again I say, Rejoice.   PHILIPPIANS 4:4

Before the mountains were brought forth, or ever thou hadst formed the earth and the world, even from everlasting to everlasting, thou art God.   PSALM 90:2

*And he said, The LORD is my rock, and my
fortress, and my deliverer;*

*The God of my rock; in him will I trust: he
is my shield, and the horn of my salvation, my
high tower, and my refuge, my saviour; thou
savest me from violence.*

*I will call on the LORD, who is worthy to be
praised: so shall I be saved from mine enemies.*

2 SAMUEL 22:2–4

*The sacrifice of the wicked is an abomination
unto the LORD: but the prayer of the upright is
his delight.* PROVERBS 15:8

*Why art thou cast down, O my soul? and why
art thou disquieted within me? hope in God: for
I shall yet praise him, who is the health of my
countenance, and my God.* PSALM 43:5

*The heavens are thine, the earth also is thine: as
for the world and the fulness thereof, thou hast
founded them.* PSALM 89:11

*And thou say in thine heart, My power and the
might of mine hand hath gotten me this wealth.*

*But thou shalt remember the LORD thy God:
for it is he that giveth thee power to get wealth,
that he may establish his covenant which he
sware unto thy fathers, as it is this day.*

DEUTERONOMY 8:17–18

And fear not them which kill the body, but are not able to kill the soul: but rather fear him which is able to destroy both soul and body in hell. MATTHEW 10:28

The fool hath said in his heart, There is no God. Corrupt are they, and have done abominable iniquity: there is none that doeth good.

PSALM 53:1

The earth is the LORD'S, and the fulness thereof; the world, and they that dwell therein.

PSALM 24:1

The LORD liveth; and blessed be my rock; and let the God of my salvation be exalted.

PSALM 18:46

My voice shalt thou hear in the morning, O LORD; in the morning will I direct my prayer unto thee, and will look up. PSALM 5:3

GOD IS ABLE

And God is able to make all grace abound toward you; that ye, always having all sufficiency in all things, may abound to every good work.

2 CORINTHIANS 9:8

The righteous cry, and the LORD heareth, and delivereth them out of all their troubles.

The LORD is nigh unto them that are of a broken heart; and saveth such as be of a contrite spirit.

Many are the afflictions of the righteous: but the LORD delivereth him out of them all.
PSALM 34:17–19

I will lift up mine eyes unto the hills, from whence cometh my help.

My help cometh from the LORD, which made heaven and earth.

He will not suffer thy foot to be moved: he that keepeth thee will not slumber.

Behold, he that keepeth Israel shall neither slumber nor sleep.

The LORD is thy keeper: the LORD is thy shade upon thy right hand.

The sun shall not smite thee by day, nor the moon by night.

The LORD shall preserve thee from all evil: he shall preserve thy soul.

The LORD shall preserve thy going out and thy coming in from this time forth, and even for evermore.
PSALM 121

Though I walk in the midst of trouble, thou wilt revive me: thou shalt stretch forth thine hand against the wrath of mine enemies, and thy right hand shall save me.

The LORD will perfect that which concerneth me: thy mercy, O LORD, endureth for ever: forsake not the works of thine own hands.

PSALM 138:7–8

For the eyes of the LORD run to and fro throughout the whole earth, to shew himself strong in the behalf of them whose heart is perfect toward him. 2 CHRONICLES 16:9

I waited patiently for the LORD; and he inclined unto me, and heard my cry.

He brought me up also out of an horrible pit, out of the miry clay, and set my feet upon a rock, and established my goings.

And he hath put a new song in my mouth, even praise unto our God: many shall see it, and fear, and shall trust in the LORD.

PSALM 40:1–3

I love the LORD, because he hath heard my voice and my supplications.

Because he hath inclined his ear unto me, therefore will I call upon him as long as I live.

The sorrows of death compassed me, and the pains of hell gat hold upon me: I found trouble and sorrow.

Then called I upon the name of the LORD;
O LORD, I beseech thee, deliver my soul.

Gracious is the LORD, and righteous; yea,
our God is merciful.

The LORD preserveth the simple: I was
brought low, and he helped me.

Return unto thy rest, O my soul; for the
LORD hath dealt bountifully with thee.

For thou hast delivered my soul from death,
mine eyes from tears, and my feet from falling.

I will walk before the LORD in the land of
the living. PSALM 116:1–9

For a just man falleth seven times, and riseth up
again. PROVERBS 24:16

Am I a God at hand, saith the LORD, and not a
God afar off? JEREMIAH 23:23

The steps of a good man are ordered by the
LORD: and he delighteth in his way.

Though he fall, he shall not be utterly cast
down: for the LORD upholdeth him with his
hand.

I have been young, and now am old; yet
have I not seen the righteous forsaken, nor his
seed begging bread. PSALM 37:23–25

Behold, I am the LORD, the God of all flesh: is there any thing too hard for me?

JEREMIAH 32:27

I, even I, am he that blotteth out thy transgressions for mine own sake, and will not remember thy sins. ISAIAH 43:25

Behold, the LORD'S hand is not shortened, that it cannot save; neither his ear heavy, that it cannot hear. ISAIAH 59:1

And Jesus looking upon them saith, With men it is impossible, but not with God: for with God all things are possible. MARK 10:27

Unless the LORD had been my help, my soul had almost dwelt in silence. PSALM 94:17

The LORD thy God in the midst of thee is mighty; he will save, he will rejoice over thee with joy; he will rest in his love, he will joy over thee with singing. ZEPHANIAH 3:17

GOD IS GRACIOUS
AND MERCIFUL

For by grace are ye saved through faith; and that not of yourselves: it is the gift of God:

Not of works, lest any man should boast.

For we are his workmanship, created in Christ Jesus unto good works, which God hath before ordained that we should walk in them.

EPHESIANS 2:8–10

Thou wilt keep him in perfect peace, whose mind is stayed on thee: because he trusteth in thee.

Trust in the LORD for ever: for in the LORD JEHOVAH is everlasting strength.

ISAIAH 26:3–4

Let not mercy and truth forsake thee: bind them about thy neck; write them upon the table of thine heart:

So shalt thou find favour and good understanding in the sight of God and man.

Trust in the LORD with all thine heart; and lean not unto thine own understanding.

In all thy ways acknowledge him, and he shall direct thy paths. PROVERBS 3:3–6

Blessed be the LORD, because he hath heard the voice of my supplications.

The LORD is my strength and my shield; my heart trusted in him, and I am helped: therefore my heart greatly rejoiceth; and with my song will I praise him.

The LORD is their strength, and he is the saving strength of his anointed.　PSALM 28:6–8

Shew thy marvellous lovingkindness, O thou that savest by thy right hand them which put their trust in thee from those that rise up against them.　PSALM 17:7

Now know I that the LORD saveth his anointed; he will hear him from his holy heaven with the saving strength of his right hand.

Some trust in chariots, and some in horses: but we will remember the name of the LORD our God.　PSALM 20:6–7

But the mercy of the LORD is from everlasting to everlasting upon them that fear him, and his righteousness to children's children;

To such as keep his covenant, and to those that remember his commandments to do them.

The LORD hath prepared his throne in the heavens; and his kingdom ruleth over all.

PSALM 103:17–19

*And he [Abraham] believed in the LORD; and
he counted it to him for righteousness.*

GENESIS 15:6

*What man is he that feareth the LORD? him
shall he teach in the way that he shall choose.
    His soul shall dwell at ease; and his seed
shall inherit the earth.
    The secret of the LORD is with them that
fear him; and he will shew them his covenant.*

PSALM 25:12–14

*Trust in the LORD, and do good; so shalt thou
dwell in the land, and verily thou shalt be fed.
    Delight thyself also in the LORD; and he
shall give thee the desires of thine heart.
    Commit thy way unto the LORD; trust also
in him; and he shall bring it to pass.
    And he shall bring forth thy righteousness as
the light, and thy judgment as the noonday.
    Rest in the LORD, and wait patiently for
him.*

PSALM 37:3–7

*And they that know thy name will put their
trust in thee: for thou, LORD, hast not forsaken
them that seek thee.*

PSALM 9:10

*But if from thence thou shalt seek the LORD thy
God, thou shalt find him, if thou seek him with
all thy heart and with all thy soul.*

*When thou art in tribulation, and all these
things are come upon thee, even in the latter
days, if thou turn to the LORD thy God, and
shalt be obedient unto his voice;*

*(For the LORD thy God is a merciful God;)
he will not forsake thee, neither destroy thee, nor
forget the covenant of thy fathers which he
sware unto them.* DEUTERONOMY 4:29–31

*The LORD is gracious, and full of compassion;
slow to anger, and of great mercy.*

*The LORD is good to all: and his tender
mercies are over all his works.*

*All thy works shall praise thee, O LORD; and
thy saints shall bless thee.* PSALM 145:8–10

*It is of the LORD'S mercies that we are not con-
sumed, because his compassions fail not.*

*They are new every morning: great is thy
faithfulness.*

*The LORD is my portion, saith my soul;
therefore will I hope in him.*

*The LORD is good unto them that wait for
him, to the soul that seeketh him.*

*It is good that a man should both hope and
quietly wait for the salvation of the LORD.*

LAMENTATIONS 3:22–26

In thee, O LORD, do I put my trust: let me never be put to confusion.

Deliver me in thy righteousness, and cause me to escape: incline thine ear unto me, and save me.

Be thou my strong habitation, whereunto I may continually resort: thou hast given commandment to save me; for thou art my rock and my fortress.   PSALM 71:1–3

As for God, his way is perfect; the word of the LORD is tried: he is a buckler to all them that trust in him.

For who is God, save the LORD? and who is a rock, save our God?

God is my strength and power: and he maketh my way perfect.

He maketh my feet like hinds' feet: and setteth me upon my high places.

He teacheth my hands to war; so that a bow of steel is broken by mine arms.

Thou hast also given me the shield of thy salvation: and thy gentleness hath made me great.

Thou hast enlarged my steps under me; so that my feet did not slip.   2 SAMUEL 22:31–37

Behold, the eye of the LORD is upon them that fear him, upon them that hope in his mercy;

To deliver their soul from death, and to keep

them alive in famine.

Our soul waiteth for the LORD: he is our help and our shield.

For our heart shall rejoice in him, because we have trusted in his holy name.

Let thy mercy, O LORD, be upon us, according as we hope in thee.   PSALM 33:18–22

In God have I put my trust: I will not be afraid what man can do unto me.   PSALM 56:11

Oh how great is thy goodness, which thou hast laid up for them that fear thee; which thou hast wrought for them that trust in thee before the sons of men!   PSALM 31:19

O give thanks unto the LORD; for he is good: because his mercy endureth for ever.

Let Israel now say, that his mercy endureth for ever.

Let the house of Aaron now say, that his mercy endureth for ever.

Let them now that fear the LORD say, that his mercy endureth for ever.

I called upon the LORD in distress: the LORD answered me, and set me in a large place.

The LORD is on my side; I will not fear: what can man do unto me?   PSALM 118:1–6

The LORD is my rock, and my fortress, and my deliverer; my God, my strength, in whom I will trust; my buckler, and the horn of my salvation, and my high tower.

I will call upon the LORD, who is worthy to be praised: so shall I be saved from mine enemies.
PSALM 18:2–3

Blessed is the man that trusteth in the LORD, and whose hope the LORD is.

For he shall be as a tree planted by the waters, and that spreadeth out her roots by the river, and shall not see when heat cometh, but her leaf shall be green; and shall not be careful in the year of drought, neither shall cease from yielding fruit.
JEREMIAH 17:7–8

The LORD is merciful and gracious, slow to anger, and plenteous in mercy.

He will not always chide: neither will he keep his anger for ever.

He hath not dealt with us after our sins; nor rewarded us according to our iniquities.

For as the heaven is high above the earth, so great is his mercy toward them that fear him.

As far as the east is from the west, so far hath he removed our transgressions from us.

Like as a father pitieth his children, so the LORD pitieth them that fear him.
PSALM 103:8–13

If my people, which are called by my name, shall humble themselves, and pray, and seek my face, and turn from their wicked ways; then will I hear from heaven, and will forgive their sin, and will heal their land. 2 CHRONICLES 7:14

In my distress I called upon the LORD, and cried to my God: and he did hear my voice out of his temple, and my cry did enter into his ears.
2 SAMUEL 22:7

With the merciful thou wilt shew thyself merciful; with an upright man thou wilt shew thyself upright;

With the pure thou wilt shew thyself pure; and with the froward thou wilt shew thyself froward.

For thou wilt save the afflicted people; but wilt bring down high looks.

For thou wilt light my candle: the LORD my God will enlighten my darkness.

For by thee I have run through a troop; and by my God have I leaped over a wall.

As for God, his way is perfect: the word of the LORD is tried: he is a buckler to all those that trust in him.

For who is God save the LORD? or who is a rock save our God?

It is God that girdeth me with strength, and maketh my way perfect.

He maketh my feet like hinds' [deer's] feet, and setteth me upon my high places.

He teacheth my hands to war, so that a bow of steel is broken by mine arms.

Thou hast also given me the shield of thy salvation: and thy right hand hath holden me up, and thy gentleness hath made me great.

Thou hast enlarged my steps under me, that my feet did not slip. PSALM 18:25–36

The LORD upholdeth all that fall, and raiseth up all those that be bowed down.

The eyes of all wait upon thee; and thou givest them their meat in due season.

Thou openest thine hand, and satisfiest the desire of every living thing.

The LORD is righteous in all his ways, and holy in all his works.

The LORD is nigh unto all them that call upon him, to all that call upon him in truth.

He will fulfil the desire of them that fear him: he also will hear their cry, and will save them.

The LORD preserveth all them that love him: but all the wicked will he destroy.

My mouth shall speak the praise of the LORD: and let all flesh bless his holy name for ever and ever. PSALM 145:14–21

Seek ye the LORD while he may be found, call ye upon him while he is near:

Let the wicked forsake his way, and the unrighteous man his thoughts: and let him return to the LORD, and he will have mercy upon him; and to our God, for he will abundantly pardon.   ISAIAH 55:6–7

Hear my prayer, O LORD, and let my cry come unto thee.
    Hide not thy face from me in the day when I am in trouble; incline thine ear unto me: in the day when I call answer me speedily.
                    PSALM 102:1–2

In the day of my trouble I will call upon thee: for thou wilt answer me.   PSALM 86:7

If I regard iniquity in my heart, the Lord will not hear me:
    But verily God hath heard me; he hath attended to the voice of my prayer.
    Blessed is God, which hath not turned away my prayer, nor his mercy from me.
                    PSALM 66:18–20

All they that see me laugh me to scorn: they shoot out the lip, they shake the head, saying,
    He trusted in the LORD that he would deliver him: let him deliver him, seeing he delighted in him.
    But thou art he that took me out of the

*womb: thou didst make me hope when I was
upon my mother's breasts.*

*I was cast upon thee from the womb: thou art
my God from my mother's belly.*   PSALM 22:7–10

Though he slay me, yet will I trust in him.
JOB 13:15

*Know therefore that the LORD thy God, he is
God, the faithful God, which keepeth covenant
and mercy with them that love him and keep his
commandments to a thousand generations.*
DEUTERONOMY 7:9

Shew me thy ways, O LORD; teach me thy paths.
*Lead me in thy truth, and teach me: for
thou art the God of my salvation; on thee do I
wait all the day.*

*Remember, O LORD, thy tender mercies and
thy lovingkindnesses; for they have been ever of
old.*   PSALM 25:4–6

*For thou, Lord, art good, and ready to forgive;
and plenteous in mercy unto all them that call
upon thee.*   PSALM 86:5

*O taste and see that the LORD is good: blessed is
the man that trusteth in him.*
O fear the LORD, ye his saints: for there is

no want to them that fear him.

The young lions do lack, and suffer hunger: but they that seek the LORD shall not want any good thing.   PSALM 34:8–10

God hath spoken once; twice have I heard this; that power belongeth unto God.

Also unto thee, O Lord, belongeth mercy: for thou renderest to every man according to his work.   PSALM 62:11–12

Likewise, I say unto you, there is joy in the presence of the angels of God over one sinner that repenteth.   LUKE 15:10

GOD'S LOVE KNOWS NO BOUNDS

Yet the LORD will command his lovingkindness in the daytime, and in the night his song shall be with me, and my prayer unto the God of my life.   PSALM 42:8

For God so loved the world, that he gave his only begotten Son, that whosoever believeth in him should not perish, but have everlasting life.   JOHN 3:16

I exhort therefore, that, first of all, supplications, prayers, intercessions, and giving of thanks, be made for all men;

For kings, and for all that are in authority; that we may lead a quiet and peaceable life in all godliness and honesty.

For this is good and acceptable in the sight of God our Saviour;

Who will have all men to be saved, and to come unto the knowledge of the truth.

1 TIMOTHY 2:1–4

Who shall separate us from the love of Christ? shall tribulation, or distress, or persecution, or famine, or nakedness, or peril, or sword?

As it is written, For thy sake we are killed all the day long; we are accounted as sheep for the slaughter.

Nay, in all these things we are more than conquerors through him that loved us.

For I am persuaded, that neither death, nor life, nor angels, nor principalities, nor powers, nor things present, nor things to come,

Nor height, nor depth, nor any other creature, shall be able to separate us from the love of God, which is in Christ Jesus our Lord.

ROMANS 8:35–39

Sing, O heavens; and be joyful, O earth; and break forth into singing, O mountains: for the LORD hath comforted his people, and will have mercy upon his afflicted.

But Zion said, The LORD hath forsaken me, and my Lord hath forgotten me.

Can a woman forget her sucking child, that she should not have compassion on the son of her womb? yea, they may forget, yet will I not forget thee. ISAIAH 49:13–15

Humble yourselves therefore under the mighty hand of God, that he may exalt you in due time:

Casting all your care upon him; for he careth for you. 1 PETER 5:6–7

For I know the thoughts that I think toward you, saith the LORD, thoughts of peace, and not of evil, to give you an expected end.

Then shall ye call upon me, and ye shall go and pray unto me, and I will hearken unto you.

And ye shall seek me, and find me, when ye shall search for me with all your heart.

JEREMIAH 29:11–13

Offer unto God thanksgiving; and pay thy vows unto the most High:

And call upon me in the day of trouble: I will deliver thee, and thou shalt glorify me.

PSALM 50:14–15

But let all those that put their trust in thee rejoice: let them ever shout for joy, because thou defendest them: let them also that love thy name be joyful in thee.

For thou, LORD, will bless the righteous; with favour wilt thou compass him as with a shield. PSALM 5:11–12

This is the day which the LORD hath made; we will rejoice and be glad in it. PSALM 118:24

Good and upright is the LORD: therefore will he teach sinners in the way.

The meek will he guide in judgment: and the meek will he teach his way.

All the paths of the LORD are mercy and truth unto such as keep his covenant and his testimonies. PSALM 25:8–10

I sought the LORD, and he heard me, and delivered me from all my fears.

They looked unto him, and were lightened: and their faces were not ashamed.

This poor man cried, and the LORD heard him, and saved him out of all his troubles.

The angel of the LORD encampeth round about them that fear him, and delivereth them.

PSALM 34:4–7

O righteous Father, the world hath not known thee: but I have known thee, and these have known that thee hast sent me.

And I have declared unto them thy name, and will declare it: that the love wherewith thou hast loved me may be in them, and I in them. JOHN 17:25–26

Are not five sparrows sold for two farthings, and not one of them is forgotten before God?

But even the very hairs of your head are all numbered. Fear not therefore: ye are of more value than many sparrows. LUKE 12:6–7

Behold, what manner of love the Father hath bestowed upon us, that we should be called the sons of God: therefore the world knoweth us not, because it knew him not.

Beloved, now are we the sons of God, and it doth not yet appear what we shall be: but we know that, when he shall appear, we shall be like him; for we shall see him as he is.

1 JOHN 3:1–2

The Lord is not slack concerning his promise, as some men count slackness; but is longsuffering to us-ward, not willing that any should perish, but that all should come to repentance.

2 PETER 3:9

Ask, and it shall be given you; seek, and ye shall find; knock, and it shall be opened unto you:

For every one that asketh receiveth; and he that seeketh findeth; and to him that knocketh it shall be opened.

Or what man is there of you, whom if his son ask bread, will he give him a stone?

Or if he ask a fish, will he give him a serpent?

If ye then, being evil, know how to give good gifts unto your children, how much more shall your Father which is in heaven give good things to them that ask him? MATTHEW 7:7–11

He sent from above, he took me, he drew me out of many waters.

He delivered me from my strong enemy, and from them which hated me: for they were too strong for me.

They prevented me in the day of my calamity: but the LORD was my stay.

He brought me forth also into a large place; he delivered me, because he delighted in me.

PSALM 18:16–19

O love the LORD, all ye his saints: for the LORD preserveth the faithful, and plentifully rewardeth the proud doer.

Be of good courage, and he shall strengthen your heart, all ye that hope in the LORD.

PSALM 31:23–24

The sacrifices of God are a broken spirit: a broken and a contrite heart, O God, thou wilt not despise.   PSALM 51:17

What shall we then say to these things? If God be for us, who can be against us?

He that spared not his own Son, but delivered him up for us all, how shall he not with him also freely give us all things?

ROMANS 8:31–32

But know that the LORD hath set apart him that is godly for himself: the LORD will hear when I call unto him.   PSALM 4:3

But if any man love God, the same is known of him.   1 CORINTHIANS 8:3

GOD GUIDES
AND PROTECTS YOU

Fear thou not; for I am with thee: be not dismayed; for I am thy God: I will strengthen thee; yea, I will help thee; yea, I will uphold thee with the right hand of my righteousness. . . .

For I the LORD thy God will hold thy right hand, saying unto thee, Fear not; I will help thee.   ISAIAH 41:10, 13

The LORD is my shepherd; I shall not want.

He maketh me to lie down in green pastures: he leadeth me beside the still waters.

He restoreth my soul: he leadeth me in the paths of righteousness for his name's sake.

Yea, though I walk through the valley of the shadow of death, I will fear no evil: for thou art with me; thy rod and thy staff they comfort me.

Thou preparest a table before me in the presence of mine enemies: thou anointest my head with oil; my cup runneth over.

Surely goodness and mercy shall follow me all the days of my life: and I will dwell in the house of the LORD for ever. PSALM 23

The law of the LORD is perfect, converting the soul: the testimony of the LORD is sure, making wise the simple.

The statutes of the LORD are right, rejoicing the heart: the commandment of the LORD is pure, enlightening the eyes.

The fear of the LORD is clean, enduring for ever: the judgments of the LORD are true and righteous altogether.

More to be desired are they than gold, yea, than much fine gold: sweeter also than honey and the honeycomb.

Moreover by them is thy servant warned: and in keeping of them there is great reward.

Who can understand his errors? cleanse thou

me from secret faults.

Keep back thy servant also from presumptu-ous sins; let them not have dominion over me: then shall I be upright, and I shall be innocent from the great transgression.

Let the words of my mouth, and the medi-tation of my heart, be acceptable in thy sight, O LORD, my strength, and my redeemer.

PSALM 19:7–14

I will instruct thee and teach thee in the way which thou shalt go: I will guide thee with mine eye. PSALM 32:8

And he said, Hearken ye, all Judah, and ye inhabitants of Jerusalem, and thou king Jehoshaphat, Thus saith the LORD unto you, Be not afraid nor dismayed by reason of this great multitude; for the battle is not your's, but God's.

To morrow go ye down against them: behold, they come up by the cliff of Ziz; and ye shall find them at the end of the brook, before the wilderness of Jeruel.

Ye shall not need to fight in this battle: set yourselves, stand ye still, and see the salvation of the LORD with you, O Judah and Jerusalem: fear not, nor be dismayed; to morrow go out against them: for the LORD will be with you.

2 CHRONICLES 20:15–17

*Then they cried unto the LORD in their trouble,
and he delivered them out of their distresses.*

*And he led them forth by the right way,
that they might go to a city of habitation.*

*Oh that men would praise the LORD for his
goodness, and for his wonderful works to the
children of men!*

*For he satisfieth the longing soul, and filleth
the hungry soul with goodness.*   PSALM 107:6–9

*And David said to Solomon his son, Be strong
and of good courage, and do it: fear not, nor be
dismayed: for the LORD God, even my God, will
be with thee; he will not fail thee, nor forsake
thee, until thou hast finished all the work for the
service of the house of the LORD.*

1 CHRONICLES 28:20

*The eternal God is thy refuge, and underneath
are the everlasting arms: and he shall thrust out
the enemy from before thee; and shall say,
Destroy them.*   DEUTERONOMY 33:27

*Through thee will we push down our enemies:
through thy name will we tread them under
that rise up against us.*

*For I will not trust in my bow, neither
shall my sword save me.*

*But thou hast saved us from our enemies,
and hast put them to shame that hated us.*

*In God we boast all the day long, and
praise thy name for ever. Selah.*   PSALM 44:5–8

*Search me, O God, and know my heart: try me,
and know my thoughts:*

*And see if there be any wicked way in me,
and lead me in the way everlasting.*

PSALM 139:23–24

*And though the Lord give you the bread of
adversity, and the water of affliction, yet shall
not thy teachers be removed into a corner any
more, but thine eyes shall see thy teachers:*

*And thine ears shall hear a word behind
thee, saying, This is the way, walk ye in it,
when ye turn to the right hand, and when ye
turn to the left.*   ISAIAH 30:20–21

*And Moses said unto the LORD, O my Lord, I
am not eloquent, neither heretofore, nor since
thou hast spoken unto thy servant: but I am
slow of speech, and of a slow tongue.*

*And the LORD said unto him, Who hath
made man's mouth? or who maketh the dumb, or
deaf, or the seeing, or the blind? have not I the
LORD?*

*Now therefore go, and I will be with thy
mouth, and teach thee what thou shalt say.*

EXODUS 4:10–12

Through God we shall do valiantly: for he it is that shall tread down our enemies.   PSALM 60:12

Then I said unto you, Dread not, neither be afraid of them.
The Lord your God which goeth before you, he shall fight for you, according to all that he did for you in Egypt before your eyes.
DEUTERONOMY 1:29–30

God is our refuge and strength, a very present help in trouble.
Therefore will not we fear, though the earth be removed, and though the mountains be carried into the midst of the sea;
Though the waters thereof roar and be troubled, though the mountains shake with the swelling thereof. Selah.   PSALM 46:1–3

There hath no temptation taken you but such as is common to man: but God is faithful, who will not suffer you to be tempted above that ye are able; but will with the temptation also make a way to escape, that ye may be able to bear it.
1 CORINTHIANS 10:13

Then the king commanded, and they brought Daniel, and cast him into the den of lions. Now the king spake and said unto Daniel, Thy God whom thou servest continually, he will deliver thee.

And a stone was brought, and laid upon the mouth of the den; and the king sealed it with his own signet, and with the signet of his lords; that the purpose might not be changed concerning Daniel.

Then the king went to his palace, and passed the night fasting: neither were instruments of musick brought before him: and his sleep went from him.

Then the king arose very early in the morning, and went in haste unto the den of lions.

And when he came to the den, he cried with a lamentable voice unto Daniel: and the king spake and said to Daniel, O Daniel, servant of the living God, is thy God, whom thou servest continually, able to deliver thee from the lions?

Then said Daniel unto the king, O king, live for ever.

My God hath sent his angel, and hath shut the lions' mouths, that they have not hurt me: forasmuch as before him innocency was found in me; and also before thee, O king, have I done no hurt.

Then was the king exceeding glad for him, and commanded that they should take Daniel up out of the den. So Daniel was taken up out of the den, and no manner of hurt was found upon him, because he believed in his God.

DANIEL 6:16–23

Be strong and of a good courage, fear not, nor be afraid of them: for the LORD thy God, he it is that doth go with thee; he will not fail thee, nor forsake thee. DEUTERONOMY 31:6

When thou passest through the waters, I will be with thee; and through the rivers, they shall not overflow thee: when thou walkest through the fire, thou shalt not be burned; neither shall the flame kindle upon thee.

For I am the LORD thy God, the Holy One of Israel, thy Saviour. ISAIAH 43:2–3

And the LORD, he it is that doth go before thee; he will be with thee, he will not fail thee, neither forsake thee: fear not, neither be dismayed. DEUTERONOMY 31:8

When thou goest out to battle against thine enemies, and seest horses, and chariots, and a people more than thou, be not afraid of them: for the LORD thy God is with thee, which brought thee up out of the land of Egypt. DEUTERONOMY 20:1

But the salvation of the righteous is of the LORD: he is their strength in the time of trouble.

And the LORD shall help them, and deliver them: he shall deliver them from the wicked, and save them, because they trust in him. PSALM 37:39–40

As for me, I will call upon God; and the LORD *shall save me.*

Evening, and morning, and at noon, will I pray, and cry aloud: and he shall hear my voice.
PSALM 55:16–17

I will both lay me down in peace, and sleep: for thou, LORD, *only makest me dwell in safety.*
PSALM 4:8

I will cry unto God most high; unto God that performeth all things for me.

He shall send from heaven, and save me from the reproach of him that would swallow me up. Selah. God shall send forth his mercy and his truth.
PSALM 57:2–3

GOD SUPPLIES YOUR NEEDS

I am the LORD *thy God, which brought thee out of the land of Egypt: open thy mouth wide, and I will fill it.*
PSALM 81:10

Blessed be the Lord, who daily loadeth us with benefits, even the God of our salvation. Selah.
PSALM 68:19

When the poor and needy seek water, and there is none, and their tongue faileth for thirst, I the LORD will hear them, I the God of Israel will not forsake them.

I will open rivers in high places, and fountains in the midst of the valleys: I will make the wilderness a pool of water, and the dry land springs of water.

I will plant in the wilderness the cedar, the shittah tree, and the myrtle, and the oil tree; I will set in the desert the fir tree, and the pine, and the box tree together:

That they may see, and know, and consider, and understand together, that the hand of the LORD hath done this, and the Holy One of Israel hath created it.   ISAIAH 41:17–20

And it shall come to pass, that before they call, I will answer; and while they are yet speaking, I will hear.   ISAIAH 65:24

Be careful for nothing; but in every thing by prayer and supplication with thanksgiving let your requests be made known to God.

And the peace of God, which passeth all understanding, shall keep your hearts and minds through Christ Jesus.   PHILIPPIANS 4:6–7

Bless the LORD, *O my soul: and all that is within me, bless his holy name.*

Bless the LORD, *O my soul, and forget not all his benefits:*

Who forgiveth all thine iniquities; who healeth all thy diseases;

Who redeemeth thy life from destruction; who crowneth thee with lovingkindness and tender mercies;

Who satisfieth thy mouth with good things; so that thy youth is renewed like the eagle's.

PSALM 103:1–5

And God said, Behold, I have given you every herb bearing seed, which is upon the face of all the earth, and every tree, in the which is the fruit of a tree yielding seed; to you it shall be for meat.

And to every beast of the earth, and to every fowl of the air, and to every thing that creepeth upon the earth, wherein there is life, I have given every green herb for meat: and it was so. GENESIS 1:29–30

Ho, every one that thirsteth, come ye to the waters, and he that hath no money; come ye, buy, and eat; yea, come, buy wine and milk without money and without price.

Wherefore do ye spend money for that which is not bread? and your labour for that which satisfieth not? hearken diligently unto me, and eat ye that which is good, and let your soul delight itself in fatness.

Incline your ear, and come unto me: hear, and your soul shall live; and I will make an everlasting covenant with you, even the sure mercies of David.   ISAIAH 55:1–3

Is any among you afflicted? let him pray. Is any merry? let him sing psalms.

Is any sick among you? let him call for the elders of the church; and let them pray over him, anointing him with oil in the name of the Lord:

And the prayer of faith shall save the sick, and the Lord shall raise him up; and if he have committed sins, they shall be forgiven him.
                                    JAMES 5:13–15

And it came to pass, that at even [evening] the quails came up, and covered the camp: and in the morning the dew lay round about the host.

And when the dew that lay was gone up, behold, upon the face of the wilderness there lay a small round thing, as small as the hoar frost on the ground.

And when the children of Israel saw it, they said one to another, It is manna: for they wist [knew] not what it was. And Moses said unto them, This is the bread which the LORD hath given you to eat.   EXODUS 16:13–15

Therefore I say unto you, Take no thought for your life, what ye shall eat, or what ye shall drink; nor yet for your body, what ye shall put on. Is not the life more than meat, and the body than raiment?

Behold the fowls of the air: for they sow not, neither do they reap, nor gather into barns; yet your heavenly Father feedeth them. Are ye not much better than they?

Which of you by taking thought can add one cubit unto his stature?

And why take ye thought for raiment? Consider the lilies of the field, how they grow; they toil not, neither do they spin:

And yet I say unto you, That even Solomon in all his glory was not arrayed like one of these.

Wherefore, if God so clothe the grass of the field, which to day is, and to morrow is cast into the oven, shall he not much more clothe you, O ye of little faith?

Therefore take no thought, saying, What shall we eat? or, What shall we drink? or, Wherewithal shall we be clothed?

(For after all these things do the Gentiles seek:) for your heavenly Father knoweth that ye have need of all these things.

But seek ye first the kingdom of God, and his righteousness; and all these things shall be added unto you.

Take therefore no thought for the morrow: for the morrow shall take thought for the things of itself. Sufficient unto the day is the evil thereof.

MATTHEW 6:25–34

But godliness with contentment is great gain.
For we brought nothing into this world, and it is certain we can carry nothing out.
And having food and raiment let us be therewith content.

1 TIMOTHY 6:6–8

For the LORD God is a sun and shield: the LORD will give grace and glory: no good thing will he withhold from them that walk uprightly.

PSALM 84:11

If ye walk in my statutes, and keep my commandments, and do them;
Then I will give you rain in due season, and the land shall yield her increase, and the trees of the field shall yield their fruit.
And your threshing shall reach unto the vintage, and the vintage shall reach unto the sowing time: and ye shall eat your bread to the full, and dwell in your land safely.
And I will give peace in the land, and ye shall lie down, and none shall make you afraid: and I will rid evil beasts out of the land, neither shall the sword go through your land.

And ye shall chase your enemies, and they shall fall before you by the sword.

And five of you shall chase an hundred, and an hundred of you shall put ten thousand to flight: and your enemies shall fall before you by the sword.

For I will have respect unto you, and make you fruitful, and multiply you, and establish my covenant with you.

And ye shall eat old store, and bring forth the old because of the new.

And I will set my tabernacle among you: and my soul shall not abhor you.

And I will walk among you, and will be your God, and ye shall be my people.

LEVITICUS 26:3–12

But my God shall supply all your need according to his riches in glory by Christ Jesus.

PHILIPPIANS 4:19

GOD IS WISE

Pride goeth before destruction, and a haughty spirit before a fall.

Better it is to be of an humble spirit with the lowly, than to divide the spoil with the proud. PROVERBS 16:18–19

Be not deceived; God is not mocked: for whatsoever a man soweth, that shall he also reap.

For he that soweth to his flesh shall of the flesh reap corruption; but he that soweth to the Spirit shall of the Spirit reap life everlasting.

And let us not be weary in well doing: for in due season we shall reap, if we faint not.

As we have therefore opportunity, let us do good unto all men, especially to them who are of the household of faith. GALATIANS 6:7–10

This book of the law shall not depart out of thy mouth; but thou shalt meditate therein day and night, that thou mayest observe to do according to all that is written therein: for then thou shalt make thy way prosperous, and then thou shalt have good success.

Have not I commanded thee? Be strong and of a good courage; be not afraid, neither be thou dismayed: for the LORD thy God is with thee whithersoever thou goest. JOSHUA 1:8–9

Let the word of Christ dwell in you richly in all wisdom; teaching and admonishing one another in psalms and hymns and spiritual songs, singing with grace in your hearts to the Lord.

And whatsoever ye do in word or deed, do all in the name of the Lord Jesus, giving thanks to God and the Father by him.

COLOSSIANS 3:16–17

When thou vowest a vow unto God, defer not to pay it; for he hath no pleasure in fools: pay that which thou hast vowed.

Better is it that thou shouldest not vow, than that thou shouldest vow and not pay.

Suffer not thy mouth to cause thy flesh to sin; neither say before the angel, that it was an error: wherefore should God be angry at thy voice, and destroy the work of thine hands?

ECCLESIASTES 5:4–6

I will set no wicked thing before mine eyes: I hate the work of them that turn aside; it shall not cleave to me.   PSALM 101:3

What? know ye not that your body is the temple of the Holy Ghost which is in you, which ye have of God, and ye are not your own?

For ye are bought with a price: therefore glorify God in your body, and in your spirit, which are God's.   1 CORINTHIANS 6:19–20

Blessed is the man whom thou chastenest, O LORD, and teachest him out of thy law;

That thou mayest give him rest from the days of adversity, until the pit be digged for the wicked.

For the LORD will not cast off his people, neither will he forsake his inheritance.

PSALM 94:12–14

These six things doth the LORD hate: yea, seven are an abomination unto him:

A proud look, a lying tongue, and hands that shed innocent blood,

An heart that deviseth wicked imaginations, feet that be swift in running to mischief,

A false witness that speaketh lies, and he that soweth discord among brethren.

PROVERBS 6:16–19

It is good for me that I have been afflicted; that I might learn thy statutes.

The law of thy mouth is better to me than thousands of gold and silver.   PSALM 119:71–72

Therefore if thou bring thy gift to the altar, and there rememberest that thy brother hath ought against thee;

Leave there thy gift before the altar, and go thy way; first be reconciled to thy brother, and then come and offer thy gift.

Agree with thine adversary quickly, whiles thou art in the way with him; lest at any time the adversary deliver thee to the judge, and the judge deliver thee to the officer, and thou be cast into prison.   MATTHEW 5:23–25

The fear of the LORD is the beginning of wisdom: and the knowledge of the holy is understanding.

PROVERBS 9:10

Honour the LORD with thy substance, and with the firstfruits of all thine increase:

So shall thy barns be filled with plenty, and thy presses shall burst out with new wine.

PROVERBS 3:9–10

My son, despise not the chastening of the LORD; neither be weary of his correction:

For whom the LORD loveth he correcteth; even as a father the son in whom he delighteth.

PROVERBS 3:11–12

Let your conversation [conduct] be without covetousness; and be content with such things as ye have: for he [Jesus] hath said, I will never leave thee, nor forsake thee.

So that we may boldly say, The Lord is my helper, and I will not fear what man shall do unto me.

HEBREWS 13:5–6

Thus saith the LORD, Let not the wise man glory in his wisdom, neither let the mighty man glory in his might, let not the rich man glory in his riches:

But let him that glorieth glory in this, that he understandeth and knoweth me, that I am the LORD which exercise lovingkindness, judgment, and righteousness, in the earth: for in these things I delight, saith the LORD.

JEREMIAH 9:23–24

Every good gift and every perfect gift is from above, and cometh down from the Father of lights, with whom is no variableness, neither shadow of turning.

Of his own will begat he us with the word of truth, that we should be a kind of firstfruits of his creatures.

Wherefore, my beloved brethren, let every man be swift to hear, slow to speak, slow to wrath:

For the wrath of man worketh not the righteousness of God.

Wherefore lay apart all filthiness and superfluity of naughtiness, and receive with meekness the engrafted word, which is able to save your souls.

But be ye doers of the word, and not hearers only, deceiving your own selves.

For if any be a hearer of the word, and not a doer, he is like unto a man beholding his natural face in a glass:

For he beholdeth himself, and goeth his way, and straightway forgetteth what manner of man he was.

But whoso looketh into the perfect law of liberty, and continueth therein, he being not a forgetful hearer, but a doer of the work, this man shall be blessed in his deed.   JAMES 1:17–25

Pleasant words are as an honeycomb, sweet to the soul, and health to the bones.

PROVERBS 16:24

Cast thy bread upon the waters: for thou shalt find it after many days. ECCLESIASTES 11:1

For whom the Lord loveth he chasteneth, and scourgeth every son whom he receiveth.

If ye endure chastening, God dealeth with you as with sons; for what son is he whom the father chasteneth not?

But if ye be without chastisement, whereof all are partakers, then are ye bastards, and not sons.

Furthermore we have had fathers of our flesh which corrected us, and we gave them reverence: shall we not much rather be in subjection unto the Father of spirits, and live?

For they verily for a few days chastened us after their own pleasure; but he for our profit, that we might be partakers of his holiness.

Now no chastening for the present seemeth to be joyous, but grievous: nevertheless afterward it yieldeth the peaceable fruit of righteousness to them which are exercised thereby.

HEBREWS 12:6–11

Favour is deceitful, and beauty is vain: but a woman that feareth the LORD, she shall be praised. PROVERBS 31:30

Now therefore fear the LORD, and serve him in sincerity and in truth: and put away the gods which your fathers served on the other side of the flood, and in Egypt; and serve ye the LORD.

And if it seem evil unto you to serve the LORD, choose you this day whom ye will serve; whether the gods which your fathers served that were on the other side of the flood, or the gods of the Amorites, in whose land ye dwell: but as for me and my house, we will serve the LORD.

JOSHUA 24:14–15

Wealth gotten by vanity shall be diminished: but he that gathereth by labour shall increase.

PROVERBS 13:11

He that hath pity upon the poor lendeth unto the LORD; and that which he hath given will he pay him again.   PROVERBS 19:17

And be ye kind one to another, tenderhearted, forgiving one another, even as God for Christ's sake hath forgiven you.   EPHESIANS 4:32

For the love of money is the root of all evil: which while some coveted after, they have erred from the faith, and pierced themselves through with many sorrows.

But thou, O man of God, flee these things; and follow after righteousness, godliness, faith, love, patience, meekness.   1 TIMOTHY 6:10–11

A soft answer turneth away wrath: but grievous words stir up anger.   PROVERBS 15:1

I beseech you therefore, brethren, by the mercies of God, that ye present your bodies a living sacrifice, holy, acceptable unto God, which is your reasonable service.
   And be not conformed to this world: but be ye transformed by the renewing of your mind, that ye may prove what is that good, and acceptable, and perfect, will of God.
                                   ROMANS 12:1–2

Behold, happy is the man whom God correcteth: therefore despise not thou the chastening of the Almighty.   JOB 5:17

Love not sleep, lest thou come to poverty; open thine eyes, and thou shalt be satisfied with bread.   PROVERBS 20:13

Let us hear the conclusion of the whole matter: Fear God, and keep his commandments: for this is the whole duty of man.   ECCLESIASTES 12:13

But I say unto you, Love your enemies, bless them that curse you, do good to them that hate you, and pray for them which despitefully use you, and persecute you;

That ye may be the children of your Father which is in heaven: for he maketh his sun to rise on the evil and on the good, and sendeth rain on the just and on the unjust.

MATTHEW 5:44–45

For every one that exalteth himself shall be abased; and he that humbleth himself shall be exalted. LUKE 18:14

Without counsel purposes are disappointed: but in the multitude of counsellors they are established.

PROVERBS 15:22

Stand fast therefore in the liberty wherewith Christ hath made us free, and be not entangled again with the yoke of bondage. GALATIANS 5:1

Poverty and shame shall be to him that refuseth instruction: but he that regardeth reproof shall be honoured. PROVERBS 13:18

For this is thankworthy, if a man for conscience toward God endure grief, suffering wrongfully.
For what glory is it, if, when ye be buffeted for your faults, ye shall take it patiently? but if, when ye do well, and suffer for it, ye take it patiently, this is acceptable with God.

1 PETER 2:19–20

Finally, my brethren, be strong in the Lord, and in the power of his might.

Put on the whole armour of God, that ye may be able to stand against the wiles of the devil.

For we wrestle not against flesh and blood, but against principalities, against powers, against the rulers of the darkness of this world, against spiritual wickedness in high places.

Wherefore take unto you the whole armour of God, that ye may be able to withstand in the evil day, and having done all, to stand.

Stand therefore, having your loins girt about with truth, and having on the breastplate of righteousness;

And your feet shod with the preparation of the gospel of peace;

Above all, taking the shield of faith, wherewith ye shall be able to quench all the fiery darts of the wicked.

And take the helmet of salvation, and the sword of the Spirit, which is the word of God:

Praying always with all prayer and supplication in the Spirit, and watching thereunto with all perseverance and supplication for all saints. EPHESIANS 6:10–18

Yet if any man suffer as a Christian, let him not be ashamed; but let him glorify God on this behalf. 1 PETER 4:16

If any of you lack wisdom, let him ask of God, that giveth to all men liberally, and upbraideth not; and it shall be given him.

But let him ask in faith, nothing wavering. For he that wavereth is like a wave of the sea driven with the wind and tossed.

For let not that man think that he shall receive any thing of the Lord.

A double minded man is unstable in all his ways.   JAMES 1:5–8

There is a way which seemeth right unto a man, but the end thereof are the ways of death.
PROVERBS 14:12

So teach us to number our days, that we may apply our hearts unto wisdom.   PSALM 90:12

Give, and it shall be given unto you; good measure, pressed down, and shaken together, and running over, shall men give into your bosom. For with the same measure that ye mete withal it shall be measured to you again.   LUKE 6:38

But we will give ourselves continually to prayer, and to the ministry of the word.   ACTS 6:4

It is better to trust in the LORD than to put confidence in man.   PSALM 118:8

*Now we know that God heareth not sinners:
but if any man be a worshipper of God, and
doeth his will, him he heareth.*　　　JOHN 9:31

*Brethren, I count not myself to have apprehended:
but this one thing I do, forgetting those things
which are behind, and reaching forth unto those
things which are before,*

　　*I press toward the mark for the prize of the
high calling of God in Christ Jesus.*

　　*Let us therefore, as many as be perfect, be
thus minded: and if in any thing ye be other-
wise minded, God shall reveal even this unto
you.*　　　PHILIPPIANS 3:13–15

*For whosoever exalteth himself shall be abased;
and he that humbleth himself shall be exalted.*
　　　LUKE 14:11

Rejoice evermore.

　　Pray without ceasing.

　　*In every thing give thanks: for this is the
will of God in Christ Jesus concerning you.*

　　Quench not the Spirit.

　　Despise not prophesyings.

　　Prove all things; hold fast that which is good.

　　Abstain from all appearance of evil.

　　*And the very God of peace sanctify you
wholly; and I pray God your whole spirit and*

soul and body be preserved blameless unto the coming of our Lord Jesus Christ.

1 THESSALONIANS 5:16–23

Wait on the LORD: be of good courage, and he shall strengthen thine heart: wait, I say, on the LORD. PSALM 27:14

GOD GIVES PROMISES TO LIVE BY

The righteous shall flourish like the palm tree: he shall grow like a cedar in Lebanon.
 Those that be planted in the house of the LORD shall flourish in the courts of our God.
 They shall still bring forth fruit in old age; they shall be fat and flourishing;
 To shew that the LORD is upright: he is my rock, and there is no unrighteousness in him.

PSALM 92:12–15

And the world passeth away, and the lust thereof: but he that doeth the will of God abideth for ever. 1 JOHN 2:17

But without faith it is impossible to please him: for he that cometh to God must believe that he is, and that he is a rewarder of them that diligently seek him. HEBREWS 11:6

Blessed is the man that walketh not in the coun-sel of the ungodly, nor standeth in the way of sinners, nor sitteth in the seat of the scornful.

But his delight is in the law of the LORD; and in his law doth he meditate day and night.

And he shall be like a tree planted by the rivers of water, that bringeth forth his fruit in his season; his leaf also shall not wither; and whatso-ever he doeth shall prosper. PSALM 1:1–3

Blessed are the poor in spirit: for theirs is the kingdom of heaven.

Blessed are they that mourn: for they shall be comforted.

Blessed are the meek: for they shall inherit the earth.

Blessed are they which do hunger and thirst after righteousness: for they shall be filled.

Blessed are the merciful: for they shall obtain mercy.

Blessed are the pure in heart: for they shall see God.

Blessed are the peacemakers: for they shall be called the children of God.

Blessed are they which are persecuted for righteousness' sake: for theirs is the kingdom of heaven.

Blessed are ye, when men shall revile you, and persecute you, and shall say all manner of evil against you falsely, for my sake.

Rejoice, and be exceeding glad: for great is your reward in heaven: for so persecuted they the prophets which were before you. MATTHEW 5:3–12

Bring ye all the tithes into the storehouse, that there may be meat in mine house, and prove me now herewith, saith the LORD of hosts, if I will not open you the windows of heaven, and pour you out a blessing, that there shall not be room enough to receive it.

And I will rebuke the devourer for your sakes, and he shall not destroy the fruits of your ground; neither shall your vine cast her fruit before the time in the field, saith the LORD of hosts. MALACHI 3:10–11

They that sow in tears shall reap in joy.

He that goeth forth and weepeth, bearing precious seed, shall doubtless come again with rejoicing, bringing his sheaves with him.

PSALM 126:5–6

And I will give them one heart, and I will put a new spirit within you; and I will take the stony heart out of their flesh, and will give them an heart of flesh:

That they may walk in my statutes, and keep mine ordinances, and do them: and they shall be my people, and I will be their God.

EZEKIEL 11:19–20

He that dwelleth in the secret place of the most High shall abide under the shadow of the Almighty.

I will say of the LORD, He is my refuge and my fortress: my God; in him will I trust.

Surely he shall deliver thee from the snare of the fowler, and from the noisome pestilence.

He shall cover thee with his feathers, and under his wings shalt thou trust: his truth shall be thy shield and buckler.

Thou shalt not be afraid for the terror by night; nor for the arrow that flieth by day;

Nor for the pestilence that walketh in darkness; nor for the destruction that wasteth at noonday.

A thousand shall fall at thy side, and ten thousand at thy right hand; but it shall not come nigh thee.

Only with thine eyes shalt thou behold and see the reward of the wicked.

Because thou hast made the LORD, which is my refuge, even the most High, thy habitation;

There shall no evil befall thee, neither shall any plague come nigh thy dwelling.

For he shall give his angels charge over thee, to keep thee in all thy ways.

They shall bear thee up in their hands, lest thou dash thy foot against a stone.

Thou shalt tread upon the lion and adder:

the young lion and the dragon shalt thou trample under feet.

Because he hath set his love upon me, therefore will I deliver him: I will set him on high, because he hath known my name.

He shall call upon me, and I will answer him: I will be with him in trouble; I will deliver him, and honour him.

With long life will I satisfy him, and shew him my salvation. PSALM 91

No weapon that is formed against thee shall prosper; and every tongue that shall rise against thee in judgment thou shalt condemn. This is the heritage of the servants of the LORD, and their righteousness is of me, saith the LORD.

ISAIAH 54:17

But I would not have you to be ignorant, brethren, concerning them which are asleep, that ye sorrow not, even as others which have no hope.

For if we believe that Jesus died and rose again, even so them also which sleep in Jesus will God bring with him.

For this we say unto you by the word of the Lord, that we which are alive and remain until the coming of the Lord shall not prevent them which are asleep.

For the Lord himself shall descend from

*heaven with a shout, with the voice of the
archangel, and with the trump of God: and the
dead in Christ shall rise first:*

*Then we which are alive and remain shall
be caught up together with them in the clouds, to
meet the Lord in the air: and so shall we ever be
with the Lord.*

*Wherefore comfort one another with these
words.*   1 THESSALONIANS 4:13–18

*He that hath an ear, let him hear what the Spirit
saith to the churches; To him that overcometh will
I give to eat of the hidden manna, and will give
him a white stone, and in the stone a new name
written, which no man knoweth saving he that
receiveth it.*   REVELATION 2:17

*Submit yourselves therefore to God. Resist the
devil, and he will flee from you.*

*Draw nigh to God, and he will draw nigh
to you.*   JAMES 4:7–8

*Him that overcometh will I make a pillar in the
temple of my God, and he shall go no more out:
and I will write upon him the name of my God,
and the name of the city of my God, which is
new Jerusalem, which cometh down out of
heaven from my God: and I will write upon
him my new name.*   REVELATION 3:12

And I will restore to you the years that the locust hath eaten, the cankerworm, and the caterpiller, and the palmerworm. JOEL 2:25

Come now, and let us reason together, saith the LORD: though your sins be as scarlet, they shall be as white as snow; though they be red like crimson, they shall be as wool. ISAIAH 1:18

He will swallow up death in victory; and the Lord GOD will wipe away tears from off all faces; and the rebuke of his people shall he take away from off all the earth: for the LORD hath spoken it. ISAIAH 25:8

Behold, I shew you a mystery; We shall not all sleep, but we shall all be changed,

In a moment, in the twinkling of an eye, at the last trump: for the trumpet shall sound, and the dead shall be raised incorruptible, and we shall be changed.

For this corruptible must put on incorruption, and this mortal must put on immortality.

So when this corruptible shall have put on incorruption, and this mortal shall have put on immortality, then shall be brought to pass the saying that is written, Death is swallowed up in victory.

O death, where is thy sting? O grave, where is thy victory? 1 CORINTHIANS 15:51–55

And I saw a new heaven and a new earth: for the first heaven and the first earth were passed away; and there was no more sea.

And I John saw the holy city, new Jerusalem, coming down from God out of heaven, prepared as a bride adorned for her husband.

And I heard a great voice out of heaven saying, Behold, the tabernacle of God is with men, and he will dwell with them, and they shall be his people, and God himself shall be with them, and be their God.

And God shall wipe away all tears from their eyes; and there shall be no more death, neither sorrow, nor crying, neither shall there be any more pain: for the former things are passed away.   REVELATION 21:1–4

Blessed is the man that endureth temptation: for when he is tried, he shall receive the crown of life, which the Lord hath promised to them that love him.

Let no man say when he is tempted, I am tempted of God: for God cannot be tempted with evil, neither tempteth he any man.

JAMES 1:12–13

And they that be wise shall shine as the brightness of the firmament; and they that turn many to righteousness as the stars for ever and ever.

DANIEL 12:3

And it shall come to pass, if thou shalt hearken diligently unto the voice of the LORD thy God, to observe and to do all his commandments which I command thee this day, that the LORD thy God will set thee on high above all nations of the earth:

And all these blessings shall come on thee, and overtake thee, if thou shalt hearken unto the voice of the LORD thy God.

Blessed shalt thou be in the city, and blessed shalt thou be in the field.

Blessed shall be the fruit of thy body, and the fruit of thy ground, and the fruit of thy cattle, the increase of thy kine, and the flocks of thy sheep.

Blessed shall be thy basket and thy store.

Blessed shalt thou be when thou comest in, and blessed shalt thou be when thou goest out.

The LORD shall cause thine enemies that rise up against thee to be smitten before thy face: they shall come out against thee one way, and flee before thee seven ways.

The LORD shall command the blessing upon thee in thy storehouses, and in all that thou settest thine hand to; and he shall bless thee in the land which the LORD thy God giveth thee.

The LORD shall establish thee an holy people unto himself, as he hath sworn unto thee, if thou shalt keep the commandments of the LORD thy God, and walk in his ways.

And all people of the earth shall see that

*thou art called by the name of the L*ORD; *and they shall be afraid of thee.*

*And the L*ORD *shall make thee plenteous in goods, in the fruit of thy body, and in the fruit of thy cattle, and in the fruit of thy ground, in the land which the L*ORD *sware unto thy fathers to give thee.*

*The L*ORD *shall open unto thee his good treasure, the heaven to give the rain unto thy land in his season, and to bless all the work of thine hand: and thou shalt lend unto many nations, and thou shalt not borrow.*

*And the L*ORD *shall make thee the head, and not the tail; and thou shalt be above only, and thou shalt not be beneath; if that thou hearken unto the commandments of the L*ORD *thy God, which I command thee this day, to observe and to do them.* DEUTERONOMY 28:1–13

For whosoever shall call upon the name of the Lord shall be saved.

How then shall they call on him in whom they have not believed? and how shall they believe in him of whom they have not heard? and how shall they hear without a preacher?

And how shall they preach, except they are sent? as it is written, How beautiful are the feet of them that preach the gospel of peace, and bring glad tidings of good things!

ROMANS 10:13–15

Sing unto the LORD, O ye saints of his, and give thanks at the remembrance of his holiness.

For his anger endureth but a moment; in his favour is life: weeping may endure for a night, but joy cometh in the morning.

PSALM 30:4–5

Cast not away therefore your confidence, which hath great recompense of reward.

For ye have need of patience, that, after ye have done the will of God, ye might receive the promise. HEBREWS 10:35–36

And I say unto you, Ask, and it shall be given you; seek, and ye shall find; knock, and it shall be opened unto you.

For every one that asketh receiveth; and he that seeketh findeth; and to him that knocketh it shall be opened.

If a son shall ask bread of any of you that is a father, will he give him a stone? or if he ask a fish, will he for a fish give him a serpent?

Or if he shall ask an egg, will he offer him a scorpion?

If you then, being evil, know how to give good gifts unto your children: how much more shall your heavenly Father give the Holy Spirit to them that ask him? LUKE 11:9–13

Jesus said unto him, If thou canst believe, all things are possible to him that believeth.

MARK 9:23

He that overcometh shall inherit all things; and I will be his God, and he shall be my son.

REVELATION 21:7

He that hath an ear, let him hear what the Spirit saith unto the churches; To him that over-cometh will I give to eat of the tree of life, which is in the midst of the paradise of God.

REVELATION 2:7

But unto you that fear my name shall the Sun of righteousness arise with healing in his wings; and ye shall go forth, and grow up as calves of the stall.   MALACHI 4:2

Henceforth there is laid up for me a crown of righteousness, which the Lord, the righteous judge, shall give me at that day: and not to me only, but unto all them also that love his appearing.   2 TIMOTHY 4:8

Cast thy burden upon the LORD, and he shall sustain thee: he shall never suffer the righteous to be moved.   PSALM 55:22

He that overcometh, the same shall be clothed in white raiment; and I will not blot out his name out of the book of life, but I will confess his name before my Father, and before his angels.

REVELATION 3:5

These things have I written unto you that believe on the name of the Son of God; that ye may know that ye have eternal life, and that ye may believe on the name of the Son of God.

And this is the confidence that we have in him, that, if we ask any thing according to his will, he heareth us:

And if we know that he hear us, whatsoever we ask, we know that we have the petitions that we desired of him. 1 JOHN 5:13–15

To him that overcometh will I grant to sit with me in my throne, even as I also overcame, and am set down with my Father in his throne.

REVELATION 3:21

Whoso offereth praise glorifieth me: and to him that ordereth his conversation [conduct] aright will I shew the salvation of God. PSALM 50:23

If we confess our sins, he is faithful and just to forgive us our sins, and to cleanse us from all unrighteousness. 1 JOHN 1:9

JESUS LIVES

For the grace of God that bringeth salvation hath appeared to all men,

Teaching us that, denying ungodliness and worldly lusts, we should live soberly, righteously, and godly, in this present world;

Looking for that blessed hope, and the glorious appearing of the great God and our Saviour Jesus Christ;

Who gave himself for us, that he might redeem us from all iniquity, and purify unto himself a peculiar people, zealous of good works.

TITUS 2:11–14

But when the fulness of the time was come, God sent forth his Son, made of a woman, made under the law,

To redeem them that were under the law, that we might receive the adoption of sons.

And because ye are sons, God hath sent forth the Spirit of his Son into your hearts, crying, Abba, Father.

Wherefore thou art no more a servant, but a son; and if a son, then an heir of God through Christ.

GALATIANS 4:4–7

Blessed be the God and Father of our Lord Jesus Christ, which according to his abundant mercy hath begotten us again unto a lively hope by the resurrection of Jesus Christ from the dead,

To an inheritance incorruptible, and undefiled, and that fadeth not away, reserved in heaven for you,

Who are kept by the power of God through faith unto salvation ready to be revealed in the last time.

Wherein ye greatly rejoice, though now for a season, if need be, ye are in heaviness through manifold temptations:

That the trial of your faith, being much more precious than of gold that perisheth, though it be tried with fire, might be found unto praise and honour and glory at the appearing of Jesus Christ:

Whom having not seen, ye love; in whom, though now ye see him not, yet believing, ye rejoice with joy unspeakable and full of glory:

Receiving the end of your faith, even the salvation of your souls. 1 PETER 1:3–9

And whatsoever ye do, do it heartily, as to the Lord, and not unto men;

Knowing that of the Lord ye shall receive the reward of the inheritance: for ye serve the Lord Christ. COLOSSIANS 3:23–24

These things I have spoken unto you, that in me ye might have peace. In the world ye shall have tribulation: but be of good cheer; I have overcome the world. JOHN 16:33

Seeing then that we have a great high priest, that is passed into the heavens, Jesus the Son of God, let us hold fast our profession.

For we have not an high priest which cannot be touched with the feeling of our infirmities; but was in all points tempted like as we are, yet without sin.

Let us therefore come boldly unto the throne of grace, that we may obtain mercy, and find grace to help in time of need. HEBREWS 4:14–16

Jesus said unto her, I am the resurrection, and the life: he that believeth in me, though he were dead, yet shall he live:

And whosoever liveth and believeth in me shall never die. Believest thou this? JOHN 11:25–26

For I know that my redeemer liveth, and that he shall stand at the latter day upon the earth:

And though after my skin worms destroy this body, yet in my flesh shall I see God. JOB 19:25–26

*Let nothing be done through strife or vainglory;
but in lowliness of mind let each esteem other
better than themselves.*

*Look not every man on his own things, but
every man also on the things of others.*

*Let this mind be in you, which was also in
Christ Jesus:*

*Who, being in the form of God, thought it
not robbery to be equal with God:*

*But made himself of no reputation, and took
upon him the form of a servant, and was made
in the likeness of men:*

*And being found in fashion as a man, he
humbled himself, and became obedient unto
death, even the death of the cross.*

*Wherefore God also hath highly exalted
him, and given him a name which is above
every name:*

*That at the name of Jesus every knee should
bow, of things in heaven, and things in earth,
and things under the earth;*

*And that every tongue should confess that
Jesus Christ is Lord, to the glory of God the
Father.* PHILIPPIANS 2:3–11

*For we have not followed cunningly devised
fables, when we made known unto you the power
and coming of our Lord Jesus Christ, but were
eyewitnesses of his majesty.* 2 PETER 1:16

Jesus Christ the same yesterday, and to day, and for ever. HEBREWS 13:8

JESUS CARES

My sheep hear my voice, and I know them, and they follow me:

And I give unto them eternal life; and they shall never perish, neither shall any man pluck them out of my hand.

My Father, which gave them to me, is greater than all; and no man is able to pluck them out of my Father's hand. JOHN 10:27–29

But whosoever will be great among you, let him be your minister;

And whosoever will be chief among you, let him be your servant:

Even as the Son of man came not to be ministered unto, but to minister, and to give his life a ransom for many. MATTHEW 20:26–28

And whatsoever ye shall ask in my name, that will I do, that the Father may be glorified in the Son.

If ye shall ask any thing in my name, I will do it. JOHN 14:13–14

Beloved, think it not strange concerning the fiery trial which is to try you, as though some strange thing happened unto you:

But rejoice, inasmuch as ye are partakers of Christ's sufferings; that, when his glory shall be revealed, ye may be glad also with exceeding joy.

If ye be reproached for the name of Christ, happy are ye; for the spirit of glory and of God resteth upon you: on their part he is evil spoken of, but on your part he is glorified.

1 PETER 4:12–14

A new commandment I give unto you, That ye love one another; as I have loved you, that ye also love one another.

By this shall all men know that ye are my disciples, if ye have love one to another.

JOHN 13:34–35

Peace I leave with you, my peace I give unto you: not as the world giveth, give I unto you. Let not your heart be troubled, neither let it be afraid. JOHN 14:27

And Jesus said unto them, I am the bread of life: he that cometh to me shall never hunger; and he that believeth on me shall never thirst.

But I said unto you, That ye also have seen me, and believe not.

All that the Father giveth me shall come to me; and him that cometh to me I will in no wise cast out.

For I came down from heaven, not to do mine own will, but the will of him that sent me.

And this is the Father's will which hath sent me, that of all which he hath given me I should lose nothing, but should raise it up again at the last day.

And this is the will of him that sent me, that every one which seeth the Son, and believeth on him, may have everlasting life: and I will raise him up at the last day.

JOHN 6:35–40

Neither pray I for these alone, but for them also which shall believe on me through their word;

That they all may be one; as thou, Father, art in me, and I in thee, that they also may be one in us: that the world may believe that thou hast sent me.

And the glory which thou gavest me I have given them; that they may be one, even as we are one:

I in them, and thou in me, that they may be made perfect in one; and that the world may know that thou hast sent me, and hast loved them, as thou hast loved me. JOHN 17:20–23

Bear ye one another's burdens, and so fulfil the law of Christ. GALATIANS 6:2

Verily I say unto you, Whatsoever ye shall bind on earth shall be bound in heaven: and whatsoever ye shall loose on earth shall be loosed in heaven.

Again I say unto you, That if two of you shall agree on earth as touching any thing that they shall ask, it shall be done for them of my Father which is in heaven.

For where two or three are gathered together in my name, there am I in the midst of them. MATTHEW 18:18–20

Behold, I stand at the door, and knock: if any man hear my voice, and open the door, I will come in to him, and will sup with him, and he with me. REVELATION 3:20

But unto every one of us is given grace according to the measure of the gift of Christ. EPHESIANS 4:7

He that hath my commandments, and keepeth them, he it is that loveth me: and he that loveth me shall be loved of my Father, and I will love him, and will manifest myself to him. JOHN 14:21

JESUS MAKES
THE DIFFERENCE

*For through him we both have access by one
Spirit unto the Father.*

*Now therefore ye are no more strangers and
foreigners, but fellowcitizens with the saints,
and of the household of God;*

*And are built upon the foundation of the
apostles and prophets, Jesus Christ himself being
the chief corner stone.* EPHESIANS 2:18–20

*For our conversation is in heaven; from whence
also we look for the Saviour, the Lord Jesus
Christ:*

*Who shall change our vile body, that it may
be fashioned like unto his glorious body, according to the working whereby he is able even to
subdue all things unto himself.*

PHILIPPIANS 3:20–21

*For whatsoever is born of God overcometh the
world: and this is the victory that overcometh
the world, even our faith.*

*Who is he that overcometh the world, but he
that believeth that Jesus is the Son of God?*

1 JOHN 5:4–5

Therefore being justified by faith, we have peace with God through our Lord Jesus Christ:

By whom also we have access by faith into this grace wherein we stand, and rejoice in hope of the glory of God.

And not only so, but we glory in tribulations also: knowing that tribulation worketh patience;

And patience, experience; and experience, hope:

And hope maketh not ashamed; because the love of God is shed abroad in our hearts by the Holy Ghost which is given unto us.

For when we were yet without strength, in due time Christ died for the ungodly.

For scarcely for a righteous man will one die: yet peradventure for a good man some would even dare to die.

But God commendeth his love toward us, in that, while we were yet sinners, Christ died for us. ROMANS 5:1–8

But the fruit of the Spirit is love, joy, peace, longsuffering, gentleness, goodness, faith,

Meekness, temperance: against such there is no law.

And they that are Christ's have crucified the flesh with the affections and lusts.

If we live in the Spirit, let us also walk in the Spirit. GALATIANS 5:22–25

Wherefore seeing we also are compassed about with so great a cloud of witnesses, let us lay aside every weight, and the sin which doth so easily beset us, and let us run with patience the race that is set before us,

Looking unto Jesus the author and finisher of our faith; who for the joy that was set before him endured the cross, despising the shame, and is set down at the right hand of the throne of God. HEBREWS 12:1–2

For this cause I bow my knees unto the Father of our Lord Jesus Christ,

Of whom the whole family in heaven and earth is named,

That he would grant you, according to the riches of his glory, to be strengthened with might by his Spirit in the inner man;

That Christ may dwell in your hearts by faith; that ye, being rooted and grounded in love,

May be able to comprehend with all saints what is the breadth, and length, and depth, and height;

And to know the love of Christ, which passeth knowledge, that ye might be filled with all the fulness of God. EPHESIANS 3:14–19

There is therefore now no condemnation to them which are in Christ Jesus, who walk not after the flesh, but after the Spirit.

For the law of the Spirit of life in Christ Jesus hath made me free from the law of sin and death. ROMANS 8:1–2

My little children, these things write I unto you, that ye sin not. And if any man sin, we have an advocate with the Father, Jesus Christ the righteous:

And he is the propitiation for our sins: and not for our's only, but also for the sins of the whole world. 1 JOHN 2:1–2

And I heard a loud voice saying in heaven, Now is come salvation, and strength, and the kingdom of our God, and the power of his Christ: for the accuser of our brethren is cast down, which accused them before our God day and night.

And they overcame him by the blood of the Lamb, and by the word of their testimony; and they loved not their lives unto the death.

REVELATION 12:10–11

I am the vine, ye are the branches. He that abideth in me, and I in him, the same bringeth forth much fruit: for without me ye can do nothing.

If a man abide not in me, he is cast forth as

a branch, and is withered; and men gather
them, and cast them into the fire, and they are
burned.

If ye abide in me, and my words abide in
you, ye shall ask what ye will, and it shall be
done unto you.

Herein is my Father glorified, that ye bear
much fruit; so shall ye be my disciples.

JOHN 15:5–8

Jesus answered and said unto them, Verily I say
unto you, If ye have faith, and doubt not, ye
shall not only do this which is done to the fig
tree, but also if ye shall say unto this mountain,
Be thou removed, and be thou cast into the sea;
it shall be done.

And all things, whatsoever ye shall ask in
prayer, believing, ye shall receive.

MATTHEW 21:21–22

And he said to them all, If any man will come
after me, let him deny himself, and take up his
cross daily, and follow me.

For whosoever will save his life shall lose it:
but whosoever will lose his life for my sake, the
same shall save it. LUKE 9:23–24

Not that I speak in respect of want: for I have learned, in whatsoever state I am, therewith to be content.

I know both how to be abased, and I know how to abound: every where and in all things I am instructed both to be full and to be hungry, both to abound and to suffer need.

I can do all things through Christ which strengtheneth me. PHILIPPIANS 4:11–13

And he said unto me, My grace is sufficient for thee: for my strength is made perfect in weakness. Most gladly therefore will I rather glory in my infirmities, that the power of Christ may rest upon me.

Therefore I take pleasure in infirmities, in reproaches, in necessities, in persecutions, in distresses for Christ's sake: for when I am weak, then am I strong. 2 CORINTHIANS 12:9–10

Blessed be the God and Father of our Lord Jesus Christ, who hath blessed us with all spiritual blessings in heavenly places in Christ:

According as he hath chosen us in him before the foundation of the world, that we should be holy and without blame before him in love:

Having predestined us unto the adoption of children by Jesus Christ to himself, according to the good pleasure of his will,

To the praise of the glory of his grace, wherein he hath made us accepted in the beloved.

In whom we have redemption through his blood, the forgiveness of sins, according to the riches of his grace;

Wherein he hath abounded toward us in all wisdom and prudence;

Having made known unto us the mystery of his will, according to his good pleasure which he hath purposed in himself:

That in the dispensation of the fulness of times he might gather together in one all things in Christ, both which are in heaven, and which are on earth; even in him:

In whom also we have obtained an inheritance, being predestinated according to the purpose of him who worketh all things after the counsel of his own will:

That we should be to the praise of his glory, who first trusted in Christ.

In whom ye also trusted, after that ye heard the word of truth, the gospel of your salvation: in whom also after that ye believed, ye were sealed with that holy Spirit of promise,

Which is the earnest of our inheritance until the redemption of the purchased possession, unto the praise of his glory.　　　EPHESIANS 1:3–14

Jesus answered and said unto her, Whosoever drinketh of this water shall thirst again:

But whosoever drinketh of the water that I shall give him shall never thirst; but the water that I shall give him shall be in him a well of water springing up into everlasting life.

JOHN 4:13–14

Therefore if any man be in Christ, he is a new creature: old things are passed away; behold, all things are become new. 2 CORINTHIANS 5:17

Beware lest any man spoil you through philosophy and vain deceit, after the tradition of men, after the rudiments of the world, and not after Christ.

For in him dwelleth all the fulness of the Godhead bodily.

And ye are complete in him, which is the head of all principality and power.

COLOSSIANS 2:8–10

The night is far spent, the day is at hand: let us therefore cast off the works of darkness, and let us put on the armour of light.

Let us walk honestly, as in the day; not in rioting and drunkenness, not in chambering and wantonness, not in strife and envying.

But put ye on the Lord Jesus Christ, and

make not provision for the flesh, to fulfil the
lusts thereof. ROMANS 13:12–14

But now in Christ Jesus ye who sometimes were
far off are made nigh by the blood of Christ.
EPHESIANS 2:13

For I am not ashamed of the gospel of Christ: for
it is the power of God unto salvation to every
one that believeth; to the Jew first, and also to
the Greek. ROMANS 1:16

Then said Jesus to those Jews which believed on
him, If ye continue in my word, then are ye my
disciples indeed;
And ye shall know the truth, and the truth
shall make you free.
They answered him, We be Abraham's seed,
and were never in bondage to any man: how
sayest thou, Ye shall be made free?
Jesus answered them, Verily, verily, I say
unto you, Whosoever committeth sin is the
servant of sin.
And the servant abideth not in the house
for ever: but the Son abideth ever.
If the Son therefore shall make you free, ye
shall be free indeed. JOHN 8:31–36

But if we walk in the light, as he is in the light, we have fellowship one with another, and the blood of Jesus Christ his Son cleanseth us from all sin.   1 JOHN 1:7

Come unto me, all ye that labour and are heavy laden, and I will give you rest.

Take my yoke upon you, and learn of me; for I am meek and lowly in heart: and ye shall find rest unto your souls.

For my yoke is easy, and my burden is light.
                    MATTHEW 11:28–30

THE HOLY SPIRIT LIVES WITHIN

Likewise the Spirit also helpeth our infirmities: for we know not what we should pray for as we ought: but the Spirit itself maketh intercession for us with groanings which cannot be uttered.

And he that searcheth the hearts knoweth what is the mind of the Spirit, because he maketh intercession for the saints according to the will of God.

And we know that all things work together for good to them that love God, to them who are the called according to his purpose.
                    ROMANS 8:26–28

I thank my God upon every remembrance of you,

Always in every prayer of mine for you all making request with joy,

For your fellowship in the gospel from the first day until now;

Being confident of this very thing, that he which hath begun a good work in you will perform it until the day of Jesus Christ.

PHILIPPIANS 1:3–6

For they that are after the flesh do mind the things of the flesh; but they that are after the Spirit the things of the Spirit.

For to be carnally minded is death; but to be spiritually minded is life and peace.

ROMANS 8:5–6

For as many as are led by the Spirit of God, they are the sons of God.

For ye have not received the spirit of bondage again to fear; but ye have received the Spirit of adoption, whereby we cry, Abba, Father.

The Spirit itself beareth witness with our spirit, that we are the children of God:

And if children, then heirs; heirs of God, and joint-heirs with Christ; if so be that we suffer with him, that we may be also glorified together.

For I reckon that the sufferings of this present time are not worthy to be compared with the glory which shall be revealed in us. ROMANS 8:14–18

*And I will pray the Father, and he shall give
you another Comforter, that he may abide with
you for ever;*

*Even the Spirit of truth; whom the world
cannot receive, because it seeth him not, neither
knoweth him: but ye know him; for he dwelleth
with you, and shall be in you.*

*I will not leave you comfortless: I will come
to you.*   JOHN 14:16–18

*But when they deliver you up, take no thought
how or what ye shall speak: for it shall be given
you in that same hour what ye shall speak.*

*For it is not ye that speak, but the Spirit of
your Father which speaketh in you.*
                                    MATTHEW 10:19–20

So then they that are in the flesh cannot please God.

*But ye are not in the flesh, but in the Spirit,
if so be that the Spirit of God dwell in you.
Now if any man have not the Spirit of Christ,
he is none of his.*

*And if Christ be in you, the body is dead
because of sin; but the Spirit is life because of
righteousness.*

*But if the Spirit of him that raised up Jesus
from the dead dwell in you, he that raised up
Christ from the dead shall also quicken your
mortal bodies by his Spirit that dwelleth in you.*
                                    ROMANS 8:8–11

But by the grace of God I am what I am: and his grace which was bestowed upon me was not in vain; but I laboured more abundantly than they all: yet not I, but the grace of God which was with me.   1 Corinthians 15:10

Wherefore I put thee in remembrance that thou stir up the gift of God, which is in thee by the putting on of my hands.

For God hath not given us the spirit of fear; but of power, and of love, and of a sound mind.
          2 Timothy 1:6–7

For the kingdom of God is not meat and drink; but righteousness, and peace, and joy in the Holy Ghost.   Romans 14:17

PART IV
WHO IS JESUS?

INTRODUCTION

The most critical element in our battle against the forces of Satan and the strongholds in our life is our relationship with Jesus Christ. All power in heaven and earth was given to Him and resides in Him.

> *And Jesus came and spake unto them, saying, All power is given unto me in heaven and in earth.* MATTHEW 28:18

Unless we are in Christ, and Christ is in us, we are helpless.

> *I am the vine, ye are the branches. He that abideth in me, and I in him, the same bringeth forth much fruit: for without me ye can do nothing.* JOHN 15:5

As mentioned earlier, if you have never made the decision to ask Jesus into your heart and committed your life to Him, maybe you are not really sure who Jesus is. You may wonder why He came to earth and whether or not He will return again. You may also question how you can get to know Him and how His power can help you defeat your strongholds. Hopefully, you will find the answer to these questions and others in the section that follows. If you have already committed your life to Christ, meditating on these words will bring new joy to your heart.

So, we say it again: Who is Jesus, and what answers can we find in the Bible?

WHO THE PROPHETS SAY HE IS

In the Old Testament, we find numerous passages of Scripture that directly or indirectly refer to Jesus Christ. Those most often quoted were written by the prophets Isaiah and Micah more than seven hundred years before Jesus' birth. Not only did they tell of His coming, but they were inspired by God to reveal the names by which He would be called and much of what He would accomplish.

As you read these prophecies, reflect on the infallibility of God in revealing the coming of Jesus the Christ hundreds of years before His appearance.

> *Therefore the Lord himself shall give you a sign; Behold, a virgin shall conceive, and bear a son, and shall call his name Immanuel.*　ISAIAH 7:14

*For unto us a child is born, unto us a son is given:
and the government shall be upon his shoulder:
and his name shall be called Wonderful,
Counsellor, The mighty God, The everlasting
Father, The Prince of Peace.*   Isaiah 9:6

*Who hath believed our report? and to whom is
the arm of the LORD revealed?*
   *For he shall grow up before him as a ten-
der plant, and as a root out of a dry ground: he
hath no form nor comeliness; and when we
shall see him, there is no beauty that we should
desire him*
   *He is despised and rejected of men; a man of
sorrows, and acquainted with grief: and we hid
as it were our faces from him; he was despised,
and we esteemed him not.*
   *Surely he hath borne our griefs, and carried
our sorrows: yet we did esteem him stricken,
smitten of God, and afflicted.*
   *But he was wounded for our transgressions,
he was bruised for our iniquities: the chastisement of our peace was upon him; and with his
stripes we are healed.*
   *All we like sheep have gone astray; we have
turned every one to his own way; and the LORD
hath laid on him the iniquity of us all.*
                              Isaiah 53:1–6

Behold, the days come, saith the LORD, that I will raise unto David a righteous Branch, and a King shall reign and prosper, and shall execute judgment and justice in the earth.

In his days, Judah shall be saved, and Israel shall dwell safely: and this is his name whereby he shall be called, THE LORD OUR RIGHTEOUSNESS. JEREMIAH 23:5–6

But thou, Bethlehem Ephratah, though thou be little among the thousands of Judah, yet out of thee shall he come forth to me that is to be ruler in Israel; whose goings forth have been from of old, from everlasting. MICAH 5:2

WHO THE ANGEL SAYS HE IS

The angel of the Lord appeared separately to both the virgin Mary and Joseph, her husband-to-be, to announce the birth of the Messiah. The Bible describes the wonder of it all.

And in the sixth month the angel Gabriel was sent from God to a city of Galilee, named Nazareth,

To a virgin espoused to a man whose name

was Joseph, of the house of David; and the virgin's name was Mary.

And the angel came in unto her, and said, Hail, thou that art highly favoured, the Lord is with thee: blessed art thou among women.

And when she saw him, she was troubled at his saying, and cast in her mind what manner of salutation this should be.

And the angel said unto her, Fear not, Mary: for thou hast found favour with God.

And, behold, thou shalt conceive in thy womb, and bring forth a son, and shalt call his name JESUS.

He shall be great, and shall be called the Son of the Highest: and the Lord God shall give unto him the throne of his father David:

And he shall reign over the house of Jacob for ever; and of his kingdom there shall be no end.

Then said Mary unto the angel, How shall this be, seeing I know not a man?

And the angel answered and said unto her, The Holy Ghost shall come upon thee, and the power of the Highest shall overshadow thee: therefore also that holy thing which shall be born of you shall be called the Son of God.

LUKE 1:26–35

But while he thought on these things, behold, the angel of the Lord appeared unto him in a dream, saying, Joseph, thou son of David, fear not to take unto thee Mary thy wife: for that which is conceived in her is of the Holy Ghost.

And she shall bring forth a son, and thou shalt call his name JESUS: for he shall save his people from their sins.　　　Matthew 1:20–21

God Incarnate

(God in the Flesh)

How amazing and humbling when we come to the realization that Almighty God Himself loves us so much that He took on the form of a man in order to accomplish His will for humankind! And He did so without in any manner or degree diminishing His divine being or nature. Only God is able to comprehend how this can be. What great and awesome meaning this brings to the name and person of Jesus Christ!

In the beginning was the Word, and the Word was with God, and the Word was God.

The same was in the beginning with God.

All things were made by him; and without him was not any thing made that was made.

In him was life; and the life was the light of men.

And the Word was made flesh, and dwelt among us, (and we beheld his glory, the glory as of the only begotten of the Father,) full of grace and truth.   JOHN 1:1–4, 14

And without controversy great is the mystery of godliness: God was manifest in the flesh, justified in the Spirit, seen of angels, preached unto the Gentiles, believed on in the world, received up into glory.   1 TIMOTHY 3:16

Jesus saith unto him, Have I been so long time with you, and yet hast thou not known me, Philip? he that hath seen me hath seen the Father.   JOHN 14:9

I and my Father are one.   JOHN 10:30

For there are three that bear record in heaven, the Father, the Word, and the Holy Ghost: and these three are one.   1 JOHN 5:7

I am Alpha and Omega, the beginning and the ending, saith the Lord, which is, and which was, and which is to come, the Almighty.   REVELATION 1:8

GOD THE SON

One explanation for the doctrine of the Trinity is found in the Westminster Shorter Catechism:

There are three persons in the Godhead, the Father, the Son, and the Holy Ghost; and these three are one God, the same in substance, equal in power and glory.

Many have tried to explain the Trinity with various analogies, but to no avail. The doctrine is beyond human understanding. But what a blessing it is to know that Jesus is God the Son!

> *And I knew him not: but he that sent me to baptize with water, the same said unto me, Upon whom thou shalt see the Spirit descending, and remaining on him, the same is he which baptizeth with the Holy Ghost.*
>
> *And I saw, and bare record that this is the Son of God.* JOHN 1:33–34

> *And Jesus, when he was baptized, went up straightway out of the water: and, lo, the heavens were opened unto him, and he saw the Spirit of God descending like a dove, and lighting upon him:*
>
> *And lo a voice from heaven, saying, This is my beloved Son, in whom I am well pleased.*
>
> MATTHEW 3:16–17

He saith unto them, But whom say ye that I am?

And Simon Peter answered and said, Thou art the Christ, the Son of the living God.

And Jesus answered and said unto him, Blessed art thou, Simon Bar-jona: for flesh and blood hath not revealed it unto thee, but my Father which is in heaven.

And I say also unto thee, That thou art Peter, and upon this rock I will build my church; and the gates of hell shall not prevail against it.

MATTHEW 16:15–18

THE LAMB OF GOD

What is meant by the term Lamb of God? The Bible states that "without shedding of blood [there] is no remission [forgiveness]" of sin (Hebrews 9:22). Before Christ's death on the cross, atonement or covering for sin was made by offering "sacrifices" of the blood of various animals to God. The blood was shed and sprinkled on the altar of the temple. When Jesus died upon the cross, He became the ultimate sacrificial Lamb. His blood was shed for the sins of all humankind once and for all. Never again would the blood of an animal be required. As the old hymn says, "Jesus paid it all. All to Him we owe."

*The next day John seeth Jesus coming unto him,
and saith, Behold the Lamb of God, which
taketh away the sin of the world.*   JOHN 1:29

*And I beheld, and I heard the voice of many
angels round about the throne and the beasts
and the elders: and the number of them was ten
thousand times ten thousand, and thousands of
thousands;*
    *Saying with a loud voice, Worthy is the
Lamb that was slain to receive power, and riches,
and wisdom, and strength, and honour, and
glory, and blessing.*
    *And every creature which is in heaven, and
on the earth, and under the earth, and such as
are in the sea, and all that are in them, heard I
saying, Blessing, and honour, and glory, and
power, be unto him that sitteth upon the throne,
and unto the Lamb for ever and ever.*
                        REVELATION 5:11–13

CHRIST THE LORD

(THE ANOINTED ONE)

*And the angel said unto them, Fear not: for,
behold, I bring you good tidings of great joy,
which shall be to all people.*

For unto you is born this day in the city of David a Saviour, which is Christ the Lord.

LUKE 2:10–11

KING OF KINGS
AND LORD OF LORDS

I give thee charge in the sight of God, who quickeneth all things, and before Christ Jesus, who before Pontius Pilate witnessed a good confession;

That thou keep this commandment without spot, unrebukeable, until the appearing of our Lord Jesus Christ:

Which in his times he shall shew, who is the blessed and only Potentate, the King of kings, and Lord of lords.   1 TIMOTHY 6:13–15

Wherefore God also hath highly exalted him, and given him a name which is above every name:

That at the name of Jesus every knee should bow, of things in heaven, and things in earth, and things under the earth;

And that every tongue should confess that Jesus Christ is Lord, to the glory of God the Father.   PHILIPPIANS 2:9–11

And I saw heaven opened, and behold a white horse; and he that sat upon him was called Faithful and True, and in righteousness he doth judge and make war.

His eyes were as a flame of fire, and on his head were many crowns; and he had a name written, that no man knew, but he himself.

And he was clothed with a vesture dipped in blood: and his name is called The Word of God.

And the armies which were in heaven followed him upon white horses, clothed in fine linen, white and clean.

And out of his mouth goeth a sharp sword, that with it he should smite the nations: and he shall rule them with a rod of iron: and he treadeth the winepress of the fierceness and wrath of Almighty God.

And he hath on his vesture and on his thigh a name written, KING OF KINGS, AND LORD OF LORDS.   REVELATION 19:11–16

HE IS ALL THINGS TO ALL MEN

Jesus truly is all things to all men for all time. Not only by His own words, but by the words of those He chose as His disciples, we see in Him all that we can ever hope for or need.

I am Alpha and Omega, the beginning and the ending, saith the Lord, which is, and which was, and which is to come, the Almighty.
REVELATION 1:8

Jesus saith unto him, I am the way, the truth, and the life: no man cometh unto the Father, but by me. JOHN 14:6

And Jesus said unto them, I am the bread of life: he that cometh to me shall never hunger; and he that believeth on me shall never thirst.
JOHN 6:35

I am the good shepherd: the good shepherd giveth his life for the sheep. JOHN 10:11

Then spake Jesus again to them, saying, I am the light of the world: he that followeth me shall not walk in darkness, but shall have the light of life. JOHN 8:12

For the law was given by Moses, but grace and truth came by Jesus Christ. JOHN 1:17

And many more believed because of his own word;
And said unto the woman, Now we believe, not because of thy saying: for we have heard him

ourselves, and know that this is indeed the
Christ, the Saviour of the world.   JOHN 4:41–42

For the Son of man is Lord even of the sabbath
day.   MATTHEW 12:8

For there is one God, and one mediator between
God and men, the man Christ Jesus.
     1 TIMOTHY 2:5

My little children, these things write I unto
you, that ye sin not. And if any man sin, we
have an advocate with the Father, Jesus Christ
the righteous:
     And he is the propitiation for our sins: and
not for our's only, but also for the sins of the
whole world.   1 JOHN 2:1–2

God, who at sundry times and in divers man-
ners spake in time past unto the fathers by the
prophets,
     Hath in these last days spoken unto us by
his Son, whom he hath appointed heir of all
things, by whom also he made the worlds;
     Who being the brightness of his glory, and
the express image of his person, and upholding all
things by the word of his power, when he had
by himself purged our sins, sat down on the right
hand of the Majesty on high.   HEBREWS 1:1–3

I Jesus have sent mine angel to testify unto you these things in the churches. I am the root and the offspring of David, and the bright and morning star. REVELATION 22:16

WHY DID
JESUS COME?

The Scriptures speak loudly and clearly!

For God so loved the world, that he gave his only begotten Son, that whosoever believeth in him should not perish, but have everlasting life.
For God sent not his Son into the world to condemn the world; but that the world through him might be saved. JOHN 3:16–17

The thief cometh not, but for to steal, and to kill, and to destroy: I am come that they might have life, and that they might have it more abundantly. JOHN 10:10

And if any man hear my words, and believe not, I judge him not: for I came not to judge the world, but to save the world. JOHN 12:47

This is a faithful saying, and worthy of all acceptation, that Christ Jesus came into the world to save sinners; of whom I am chief.
1 TIMOTHY 1:15

For the Son of man is come to save that which was lost. MATTHEW 18:11

For I am not come to call the righteous, but sin-
ners to repentance.   MATTHEW 9:13

For this purpose the Son of God was manifested,
that he might destroy the works of the devil.
                                    1 JOHN 3:8

The Spirit of the Lord is upon me, because he
hath anointed me to preach the gospel to the
poor; he hath sent me to heal the brokenhearted,
to preach deliverance to the captives, and recov-
ering of sight to the blind, to set at liberty them
that are bruised,
*   To preach the acceptable year of the Lord.*
*   And he closed the book, and he gave it again*
to the minister, and sat down. And the eyes of
all them that were in the synagogue were fas-
tened on him.
*   And he began to say to them, This day is*
this scripture fulfilled in your ears.
                                    LUKE 4:18–21

And we have seen and do testify that the Father
sent the Son to be the Saviour of the world.
                                    1 JOHN 4:14

Wherefore he is able also to save them to the
uttermost that come unto God by him, seeing he
ever liveth to make intercession for them.
                                    HEBREWS 7:25

*But God commendeth his love toward us, in that,
while we were yet sinners, Christ died for us.*
ROMANS 5:8

*So Christ was once offered to bear the sins of
many.* HEBREWS 9:28

*Grace be to you and peace from God the Father,
and from our Lord Jesus Christ,
      Who gave himself for our sins, that he
might deliver us from this present evil world,
according to the will of God and our Father.*
GALATIANS 1:3–4

*These things have I spoken unto you, that my
joy might remain in you, and that your joy
might be full.* JOHN 15:11

WILL JESUS COME AGAIN?

As before, the Scripture is loud and clear!

> *Let not your heart be troubled: ye believe in God, believe also in me.*
>
> *In my Father's house are many mansions: if it were not so, I would have told you. I go to prepare a place for you.*
>
> *And if I go and prepare a place for you, I will come again, and receive you unto myself; that where I am, there ye may be also.*
>
> JOHN 14:1–3

> *And when he had spoken these things, while they beheld, he was taken up; and a cloud received him out of their sight.*
>
> *And while they looked stedfastly toward heaven as he went up, behold, two men stood by them in white apparel;*
>
> *Which also said, Ye men of Galilee, why stand ye gazing up into heaven? this same Jesus, which is taken up from you into heaven, shall so come in like manner as ye have seen him go into heaven.*
>
> ACTS 1:9–11

> *For the Son of man shall come in the glory of his Father with his angels.*
>
> MATTHEW 16:27

Therefore be ye also ready: for in such an hour as ye think not the Son of man will come.

MATTHEW 24:44

When the Son of man shall come in his glory, and all the holy angels with him, then shall he sit upon the throne of his glory.

MATTHEW 25:31

For the Lord himself shall descend from heaven with a shout, with the voice of the archangel, and with the trump [trumpet] of God: and the dead in Christ shall rise first:

Then we which are alive and remain shall be caught up together with them in the clouds, to meet the Lord in the air: and so shall we ever be with the Lord. 1 THESSALONIANS 4:16–17

He which testifieth these things saith, Surely I come quickly. Amen. Even so, come, Lord Jesus.

REVELATION 22:20

How May I Know Him?

Without a doubt, the greatest stronghold Satan can place in a person's life is a spirit of unbelief in Jesus Christ and a refusal to accept the gift of forgiveness of sins and eternal life. When we accept Him as our Lord and Savior, we are adopted as children of God.

As has been stated, without this relationship with Christ, not only are we powerless to defeat the works of the devil, we are also lost for all eternity. But to know Him, to love Him, and to have Him in us and we in Him is to have it all (see John 17:20–23).

The need for Jesus is well established. However, for various reasons, there are many who choose to reject Him and all that He offers. Many others recognize their need for a Savior but don't know how to know Him. To begin, let's examine why and how men and women arrived at the condition of needing a Savior and how God has responded to that need. To do so, we will use what is known as the "Heller Illustration," shown on the following pages.

In the beginning there was God, and God was holy. God created the heavens and the earth and all that is in it. He then created Adam and

Eve (represented by the stick people in figure 1).

In reality God created two Adams all in one person and two Eves all in one person. He created physical Adam and physical Eve (represented by the P's) and He also created spiritual Adam and spiritual Eve (represented by the S's in figure 1). The Spirit of God—the very life of God—was in both Adam and Eve. They had physical life and they had spiritual life.

At first Adam and Eve had a perfect relationship with God. They were enjoying God and He was pleased with His creation.

God gave Adam and Eve instructions how they were to care for their surroundings in the Garden of Eden. In this environment of almost total freedom, God placed only one restriction on Adam and Eve. He commanded them not to eat the fruit from one tree, the Tree of the Knowledge of Good and Evil. He told them that if they disobeyed, they would surely die.

Despite God's command to Adam and Eve and the warning He gave them, the serpent (Satan) was successful in convincing Eve that God hadn't meant what He said. In fact, Satan assured them, if they ate from the forbidden tree, they would be like gods.

As we know, first Eve and then Adam did eat of the forbidden fruit in defiance of God.

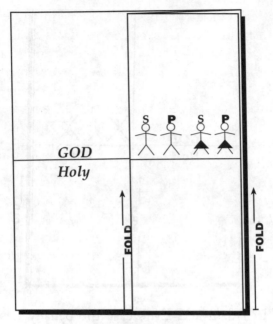

Figure 1
*Many like to share these illustrations with a
friend. To do so, begin by using an 8½" by 11"
sheet of paper folded as shown in the diagram.*

When Adam and Eve disobeyed God, for the
first time *sin* entered the world. Sin is any thought
or action not in accordance with the will or the
commandments of God. God is a loving God, but
He also is a just God, and it is a just God's law that
demands a penalty for sin (figure 2).

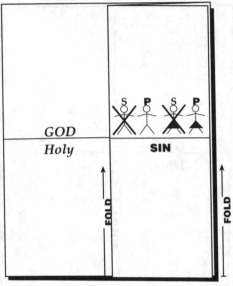

Figure 2

In Adam and Eve's case the penalty was inflicted. God withdrew His life from them, and they died—spiritually! X's have been placed over both Adam and Eve to denote their spiritual death.

Death always involves separation. The result of physical death is the separation of the human spirit from the body. Spiritual death results in a person being separated from God.

Because of Adam and Eve's sin, not only did they die spiritually, but Adam and Eve became separated from God (figure 3).

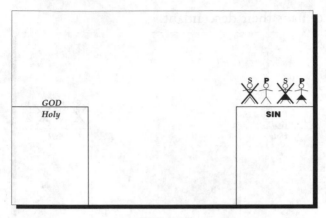

Figure 3

It was as though a huge chasm had opened with God on one side and "man" completely isolated from God on the other.

When "man" (Adam and Eve) yielded to Satan's urging, "man" acquired a sin nature and became a servant of sin, or a servant of Satan. A holy God had no choice but to distance Himself from His human creation. "Man" was now spiritually dead and separated from God.

Following their separation from God and ejection from the Garden of Eden, Adam and Eve began to have children. First came Cain and then Abel and then many more. Since that time, millions upon millions of people have been physically born—and it all began with Adam and Eve. Each of us is their descendant.

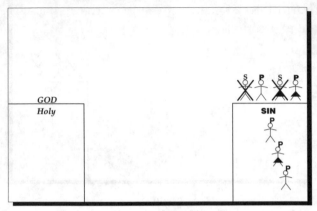

Figure 4

Note that there is a P above each descendant stick figure to emphasize that each of us enters this world with physical life only. We can inherit many physical characteristics, but we cannot inherit spiritual life. It must be given by God. We are born physically alive but spiritually dead.

In addition, we all arrive with the same sin nature Adam and Eve acquired when they listened to Satan and disobeyed God.

Because we were created by God in His image, we have an inner longing for God. It has been said that deep in the heart of every human being is the consciousness of God. Blaise Pascal, the renowned French physicist and philosopher, called that longing "a God-shaped vacuum in the heart of every man." In figure 5, the hearts with the white circles depict that vacuum.

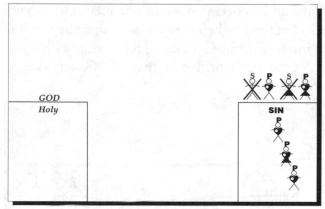

Figure 5

God created man for His own enjoyment and to have a personal relationship with Him. This relationship was destroyed by man through sin, but the desire for God still exists in the heart of each human being. It's a void that many have tried to fill with money, alcohol, drugs, sex, and various pursuits, all to no avail. This void can be filled only by God Himself.

Because of our God-consciousness and the need to fill the vacuum caused by our separation from God, we try in many ways to come to Him. We attempt to get from our side of the chasm to

His side by building what we will call "human effort bridges."

There are many human effort bridges. Most have an important place in our relationship with God but only when they are no longer the result of human effort but a renewed fellowship with Him.

One such bridge is that of "Good Works" (figure 6).

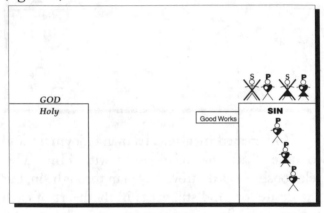

Figure 6

There is no question but what God wants us to do good things for other people—and for Him. But our good deeds should be the natural result of a right relationship with God and not a means of trying to reach Him. He is not influenced by our human effort bridges of good works, and they will never get us into heaven, as some believe.

Another bridge many rely on to reach God is "Religion" (figure 7).

There is now and always has been misunderstanding concerning the meaning of the word *religion*. For purposes of discussion, we would define religion as a human-made system for relating to God or a god of some type.

There are many such religions that captivate the hearts and minds of men and women but in no way bring them any closer to Almighty God. Many people are religious, but far fewer are spiritually religious.

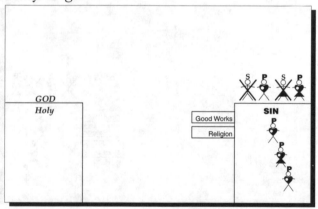

Figure 7

Although such religions are initiated by men, in actuality they are fostered by Satan with one purpose: to make us antagonistic toward and draw us away from the true plan of God. Generally, these religions are good works oriented and closely related to the first bridge. Religion without the Spirit of God is an exercise in futility and an affront to God.

A third bridge is "Church Membership" and "Church Attendance" (figure 8).

Sad to say, but there are far too many people gracing the pews of our churches who are relying solely upon church membership and church attendance to bridge the gap between themselves and God.

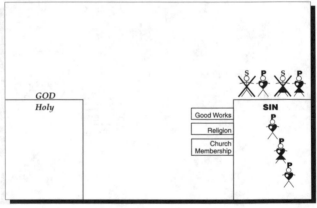

Figure 8

If you were to question these church members on why they should be allowed into heaven, many would respond that they attend church regularly, maybe teach a Sunday school class, sing in the choir, or support the church in other ways.

Church involvement is of the utmost importance to a closer walk with God, but erroneously motivated church activity will never get the job done. It may impress other people, but it does not impress God.

Although the next bridge of "Baptism" is also of great importance to each person's walk with God, in and of itself it is not a means of reaching Him (figure 9). Rather, baptism is an outward and visible sign of something far greater than just a tradition supposedly designed to bring us to God. As our illustration develops, we will find the true meaning, and we will better understand that when baptism is used as a human-made method to span the breach, it too falls far short of the mark.

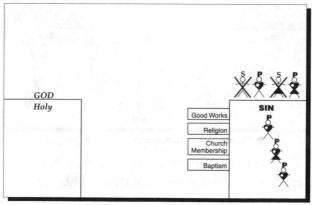

Figure 9

When we rely on these bridges and other things to bring us to God, we place our faith in them rather than where God would have it placed—in Him. We make these things and other pursuits the gods of our lives rather than God Himself. When we end our physical lives on this earth still separated from God and spiritually dead because of trusting *our* ways of reaching Him, the only result will be *hell!*

And do you know what hell is? Total separation from God. . .in total darkness. . .under perpetual torment. . .in a burning lake of fire. . . without hope. . .forever and ever!

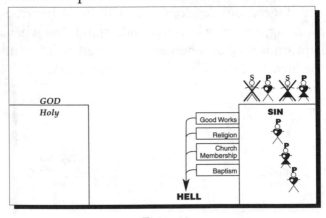

Figure 10

Imagine spending eternity in one of the conditions described, let alone all of them. The Bible says that those who are in hell will beg to die but will not be able to. How sad—and how unnecessary!

It is not God's desire that any person should spend eternity in hell. He wants all men and women to receive spiritual life and spend eternity with Him.

Because of His immeasurable *Love* for us, His great *Mercy,* and His *Amazing Grace,* God has *His Plan* for us to come to Him. And that plan is found in *Jesus Christ!* (See figure 11.)

> *Jesus saith unto him, I am the way, the truth and the life: no man cometh unto the Father, but by me.* JOHN 14:6

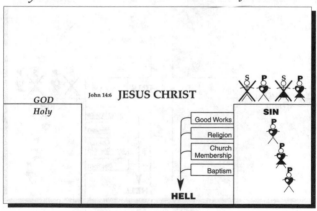

Figure 11

Jesus did not say that "Good Works" is the way; that any "Religion" is the answer; that "Church

Membership" guarantees salvation; that "Baptism" is the solution; or that any other god, guru, or human-made method of any kind will fit the bill. Jesus said, "I AM THE WAY."

God the Son became the bridge. . .the only bridge to end the sin separation between God and man.

And how did Jesus become this bridge? By shedding His blood upon the cross to pay the penalty for our sins. The Bible tells us that "Christ also hath once suffered for sins, the just for the unjust, that he might bring us to God" (1 Peter 3:18, figure 12).

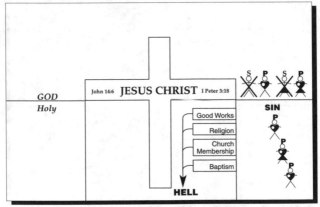

Figure 12

Previously we discussed the meaning of the Lamb of God and that only blood can bring us forgiveness for our sins and cleanse us from them.

We mentioned that before Christ's ultimate sacrifice, the blood of lambs and other animals were offered as sacrifices to "cover" sin. Their blood was shed. But God, in His love and mercy, offered Himself as one final sacrifice for all time.

Because of Jesus Christ, and Him only, we can move from a position of spiritual death and separation from God to the relationship with Him that He longs for. And when we do, several things occur.

First, we are born again, sin free! When we come to God through Christ, we receive spiritual life, the same sin-free God life that was given to Adam and Eve. Man was spiritually born once, but he died because of sin. If he is spiritually born a second time, he is born again. As the new stick figures show in figure 13, he now has both physical life and spiritual life.

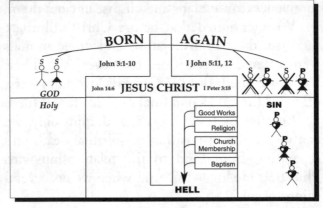

Figure 13

Do you remember Jesus' encounter with Nicodemus the Pharisee? In that exchange, Jesus said, "Except a man be born again, he cannot see the kingdom of God" (John 3:3). Later in the Bible, the disciple John writes again of this new life in Christ: "And this is the record, that God hath given to us eternal life, and this life is in his Son. He that hath the Son hath life; and he that hath not the Son of God hath not life" (1 John 5:11–12).

Along with our spiritual rebirth is the filling of the God-shaped vacuum in our hearts. No longer is there an empty void. As the stick figures depict in figure 14, such a space is filled by God the Spirit. At the very moment we are born again, the Holy Spirit comes to dwell within us. His presence fully satisfies the longing in our hearts.

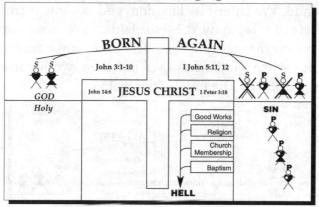

Figure 14

Before Jesus ascended into heaven, He made a promise: "And I will pray the Father, and he shall give you another Comforter, that he may abide with you for ever; Even the Spirit of truth; whom the world cannot receive, because it seeth him not, neither knoweth him: but ye know him; for he dwelleth with you, and shall be in you" (John 14:16–17).

The Comforter is the Holy Spirit, the third person of the Godhead—God the Father; God the Son; and God the Holy Spirit. He is real. He is a person. He dwells within and guides each Christian.

It is now God's pleasure to open His arms

and hold each of us close to Him as His adopted child. We enter His kingdom and become members of His family, the Jesus family. We arrive and live on this earth as members of a people family. But when God takes over our lives, we become members of His family (figure 15).

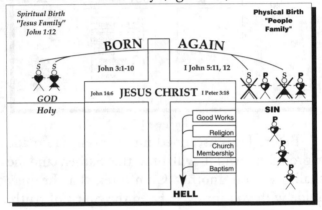

Figure 15

But as many as received him [Jesus], to them gave he power to become the sons [children] of God, even to them that believe on his name.

JOHN 1:12

Lest you doubt your family standing after being born again, consider these verses.

The Spirit itself beareth witness with our spirit, that we are the children of God: And if children,

then heirs; heirs of God, and joint-heirs with
Christ. ROMANS 8:16–17

Let's look again at the four bridges previously discussed.

When we enter into the new relationship with God, we find that we no longer have to strive to reach God through some human-made device. We are with Him and He with us. We are His! We have crossed the chasm; the separation is ended.

And now the things that were once bridges take on a whole new meaning. The lines on figure 16 show that these former bridges are now related to God rather than separating us from Him.

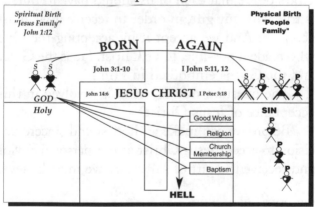

Figure 16

Our "Good Works" are no longer humanly "good" but divinely "good." Our "Religion" is now

Christianity, a relationship between us and Jesus Christ. "Church Membership" is fellowship with others with Christ as the center of attention. And "Baptism" is an outward and visible sign of our identification with Him.

All the benefits that we have described are not "automatically" given. That Jesus died for our sins does not mean that everyone is saved.

Salvation is a free gift from God. It cannot be earned. It cannot be purchased. It cannot be taken without the "Owner's" consent. It can be received only as an unearned, undeserved gift. It is available to every person born into this world, and it is God's desire that each of us should have it. But, as is true with any gift, in order to receive it we must accept it. And we accept it by accepting the One who made it possible, Jesus Christ. He is the Giver and the Gift is embodied in Him.

The question now is, what is involved in this acceptance of Jesus Christ?

Before we can make an honest and sincere decision to accept Jesus Christ as our personal Savior and receive the gift of salvation, we must believe.

To Believe

*Believe on the Lord Jesus Christ, and thou shalt
be saved.*   Acts 16:31

There are many who know the things we have discussed, but their knowledge does not come from
the heart. Heart belief is what is lacking, and is
what sets the Christian apart from others in this
world.

In accepting Christ, we must believe in Him
with all our hearts and without reservation. We
believe that He is the Son of God; that He died
on the cross for our sins; that He rose from the
dead and ascended into heaven; that He will come
again to receive into His kingdom those who
have trusted Him and judge those who have rejected Him. We believe enough to place our lives
completely under His control and in His keeping.
So, after being certain of our belief, we need to
repent.

To Repent

From that time Jesus began to preach, and to say, Repent: for the kingdom of heaven is at hand.　　　　　　　　MATTHEW 4:17

The first step in repentance is to realize that we are sinners: "For all have sinned, and come short of the glory of God" (Romans 3:23).

It may be difficult for someone who has led a reasonably "good" life and never intentionally harmed anyone or committed any "major" sins to say, "I am a sinner." We must realize that all have sinned, and repent and seek forgiveness.

The New Testament word *repent* is an English translation of the Greek word *metanoia—meta* meaning "change" and *noia* meaning "mind." It also means "to turn." When we fully repent, we change our minds. We make a decision to turn from following the ways of the world to following Jesus. No longer do we walk away from Him. We walk with Him.

This repenting, this turning and joining Christ, involves a willful decision based on our believing in Him. It is not something someone else can do for us. It is solely between us and the Lord Jesus. It prepares us for our next step in finding Him—to confess.

To Confess

That if thou shalt confess with thy mouth the Lord Jesus, and shalt believe in thine heart that God hath raised him from the dead, thou shalt be saved.

For with the heart man believeth unto righteousness; and with the mouth confession is made unto salvation. ROMANS 10:9–10

With our mouths we confess or affirm our belief and trust in Jesus Christ and our decision to repent and follow Him.

Our verbal confession should first be made to Jesus Himself. If we have believed and repented, and it is our desire to ask Him into our hearts, all we need do is tell Him. We can confess our sins to Him and ask for His forgiveness. We can tell Him we believe He truly is the Son of God and died for our sins and rose again. We can tell Him we want to commit our lives to Him, and we can thank Him for being our Savior.

We have all heard the expression, "Confession is good for the soul." To this should be added, confession will save the soul!

WHERE ARE YOU?

Are you on God's side of the chasm. . .born again
. . .forgiven of your sins. . .indwelt by the Holy
Spirit. . .adopted as a child of God and experiencing the joy of your salvation and the assurance
of eternal life with Christ Jesus?

Or are you with most of the world, still separated from God, without spiritual life, and in dan-
ger of spending eternity separated from God and
suffering the consequences of declining the greatest gift you could ever receive? (See figure 17.)

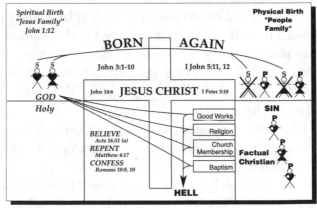

Figure 17

If your answer to the last question is in the affir-
mative, I encourage you to open the door of your
heart to Jesus now. Listen to Jesus speaking to you:

*Behold, I stand at the door and knock: if any
man hear my voice, and open the door, I will
come in to him, and will sup with him, and he
with me.*   REVELATION 3:20

It doesn't matter what your present condition
might be or what horrible things you may have
done in your lifetime. If you are sincere in your
desire to turn your life over to Him, Jesus will
accept you just as you are and forgive every sin
you have committed.

If you are ready to issue an invitation to Jesus,
you can welcome Him in your own words or pray
this prayer of submission:

*Lord Jesus,
I know that I am a sinner. I truly repent of my
sins and ask for Your forgiveness. I believe in my
heart that You are the Son of God and that You
died on the cross and paid the penalty for my sins
with Your shed blood. I want to surrender my
life to You. I ask You to come into my heart and
take control of my life. Thank You for forgiving
me, and for becoming my Savior and my Lord.*

If you sincerely prayed that prayer or one similar to it just now or at any time in the past, you
can join with the whole family of God in claim-
ing a positive answer to the next question.

CAN JESUS DESTROY MY STRONGHOLDS?

If you are walking hand in hand with our Lord Jesus Christ and living your life for Him, the answer to the above question is a resounding YES! You can count on Him to destroy any and all of your strongholds. With Jesus by your side, you can live in victory. Before we consider the implications of that statement, let's look at several promises Jesus made:

- He will give you rest from life's cares (Matthew 11:28).
- He will never leave you or forsake you (Hebrews 13:5).
- He will always provide spiritual enlightenment and answers, and He will always come into your heart—all you have to do is ask (Matthew 7:7–8).
- He will speak on your behalf before God (Matthew 10:32).
- He came to destroy the works of the devil (1 John 3:8).
- His Word and promises will last forever (Matthew 24:35).

These are just several of the many promises Jesus made that assure us of His love and compassion and of His help in our times of need.

In addition to His words, His ability to come to our aid is proven by what He has already done. All we need do is look at the numerous passages of Scripture that describe the many miracles He performed because of how much He cared for hurting people.

But now He is in heaven, sitting at the right hand of God the Father. How then can He fight the enemy for us and with us? He does so through His name, through His blood, through His intercession, and through His Holy Spirit.

THROUGH HIS NAME

We have discussed the power of Jesus' name as one of our spiritual weapons. His name remains as indomitable today as ever, and He continues to encourage us to use it as one of our principal weapons.

And whatsoever ye shall ask in my name, that will I do, that the Father may be glorified in the Son. If ye shall ask any thing in my name, I will do it. JOHN 14:13–14

However, we must always exercise caution not to allow the name of Jesus to be used as a magical incantation or mantra. What we are saying when we repeat the words, "in Jesus' name" is "under the authority and in the power of Jesus." This authority is granted only to those who believe in Jesus and who are walking in obedience to Him. This authority is not indiscriminately given, nor should it be lightly used.

Wherefore God also hath highly exalted him, and given him a name which is above every name: That at the name of Jesus every knee should bow, of things in heaven, and things in earth, and things under the earth; And that every tongue should confess that Jesus Christ is Lord, to the glory of God the Father.

PHILIPPIANS 2:9–11

THROUGH HIS BLOOD

Again, we have talked about the power of the blood and what a force it is as a weapon against the powers of darkness. The blood of the Lamb is always effective against Satan and his demons when applied in faith by a believer cleansed from sin.

(See Psalm 66:18 and 1 John 1:9.) It will always bring deliverance. Jesus' blood will never fail because He cannot fail!

When Jesus shed His blood upon the cross, to those standing by it appeared to be ordinary blood. But the life and power of God was in that blood. It was this power that defeated sin and Satan and made it possible for you and me to be redeemed by the blood of the Lamb.

When we "apply" or "plead the blood," we are by Christ's authority applying His invincible power.

THROUGH HIS INTERCESSION

One of the most overlooked ways in which Jesus shows His love and compassion for us is by interceding with the Heavenly Father on our behalf. Jesus is in a perfect position to do so because He sits at the right hand of the Father upon His throne of grace.

> *God, who at sundry times and in divers manners spake in time past unto the fathers by the prophets,*
>
> *Hath in these last days spoken unto us by his Son, whom he hath appointed heir of all*

things, by whom also he made the worlds;

Who being the brightness of his glory, and the express image of his person, and upholding all things by the word of his power, when he had by himself purged our sins, sat down on the right hand of the Majesty on high.

HEBREWS 1:1–3

Wherefore he is able also to save them to the uttermost that come unto God by him, seeing he ever liveth to make intercession for them.

HEBREWS 7:25

Intercession means to beg or to plead on behalf of another. Can you see it? Can you feel it? Jesus our Lord sitting at the right hand of God Almighty, pleading for you! How utterly awesome!

THROUGH HIS HOLY SPIRIT

Before Jesus ascended into heaven following His crucifixion and resurrection, He promised that He would not leave His people alone without His presence. How can this be? He was leaving and yet He would still be there? Again, we turn to the Scriptures for the answer.

And I will pray the Father, and he shall give
you another Comforter, that he may abide with
you for ever;

Even the Spirit of truth; whom the world
cannot receive, because it seeth him not, neither
knoweth him: but ye know him; for he dwelleth
with you, and shall be in you.

I will not leave you comfortless: I will come
to you.   JOHN 14:16–18

AND WHO IS
THE COMFORTER?

But the Comforter, which is the Holy Ghost,
whom the Father will send in my name, he shall
teach you all things, and bring all things to your
remembrance, whatsoever I have said unto you.
                                           JOHN 14:26

Jesus said that the Comforter, who is the Holy
Spirit, would come, and then He states that He,
Jesus, would come. Again we ask, how can this
be? Scripture, as always, has the answer.

For there are three that bear record in heaven,
the Father, the Word, and the Holy Ghost: and
these three are one.   1 JOHN 5:7

By virtue of the "oneness" of the Trinity, Jesus is with us in the person of the Holy Spirit (see also John 1:1–2, 14). When we accept Christ as our Savior, He lives in us by His Spirit, who blesses us with many of His ministries:

- He exercises control over us, if we open our hearts to Him.
- He empowers and equips us with the weapons of our warfare.
- He restrains evil and keeps those who rebel against God from becoming victorious. Without the work of the Holy Spirit, this world would be much worse.
- He convicts us of sin. The Holy Spirit lets us know when what we are doing or thinking is right and when it is wrong.
- He reveals Jesus Christ to us (see John 16:7–14).
- We bear His fruit of love, joy, peace, patience, gentleness, goodness, faith, meekness, and temperance (see Galatians 5:22–23).

Yes, the Holy Spirit is always active on our behalf, and Jesus, through this same Spirit, His powerful name, His shed blood, and His intercession is more than able to destroy the strongholds of this world. Through Him we can live in victory.

CONCLUSION

The contents and purpose of this book may best be summed up in these words written by the apostle Paul:

> *Therefore being justified by faith, we have peace with God through our Lord Jesus Christ:*
> *By whom also we have access by faith into this grace wherein we stand, and rejoice in hope of the glory of God.*
> *And not only so, but we glory in tribulations also: knowing that tribulation worketh patience;*
> *And patience experience, and experience hope:*
> *And hope maketh not ashamed; because the love of God is shed abroad in our hearts by the Holy Ghost which is given unto us.*
>
> ROMANS 5:1–5

It is my prayer that this book has been a message of hope. . .hope in the power of praise and worship; hope in the power of prayer; hope in the power of the Word of God; hope in the power of the name of Jesus; hope in the power of the blood of the Lamb; and hope in the love, compassion, grace, and mercy of God the Father, God the Son, and God the Holy Spirit.

> *Eye hath not seen, nor ear heard, neither have entered into the heart of man, the things which God hath prepared for them that love him.*
>
> 1 CORINTHIANS 2:9

ABOUT THE AUTHORS

CLARENCE L. BLASIER lives in North Canton, Ohio, where he is a charter member of The Chapel in North Canton and active in the church's evangelism training and various outreach ministries.

He has an extensive business and public service background and has held prominent local, state, and national civic organization offices.

The owner of Matthew Publishing Company, Blasier is also the author of several best-selling Christian books:

Bible Answers for Every Need
God's Encouraging Word
What To Believe and Why
May I Share Something with You
Someone Once Shared with Me?
The Golden Treasury of Bible Wisdom

REX W. MARSHALL is a member of The Chapel in North Canton, and is actively pursuing training and ministry outreach opportunities in the field of pastoral counseling.

Inspirational Library

Beautiful purse/pocket-size editions of Christian classics b
in flexible leatherette. These books make thoughtful gif
everyone on your list, including yourself!

When I'm on My Knees   The highly popular
collection of devotional thoughts on prayer,
especially for women.
Flexible Leatherette. $4.97

The Bible Promise Book   Over 1,000 prom-
ises from God's Word arranged by topic. What
does God promise about matters like: Anger,
Illness, Jealousy, Love, Money, Old Age, and
Mercy? Find out in this book!
Flexible Leatherette. $3.97

Daily Wisdom for Women   A daily devotional
for women seeking biblical wisdom to apply to
their lives. Scripture taken from the New
American Standard Version of the Bible.
Flexible Leatherette. $4.97

My Daily Prayer Journal   Each page is dated
and features a Scripture verse and ample room
for you to record your thoughts, prayers, and
praises. One page for each day of the year.
Flexible Leatherette. $4.97

Available wherever books are sold.
Or order from:

Barbour Publishing, Inc.
P.O. Box 719
Uhrichsville, OH 44683
http://www.barbourbooks.com

If you order by mail, add $2.00 to your order for shipping.
Prices are subject to change without notice.